SWARM INTELLIGENCE

SWARM INTELLIGENCE

WHAT NATURE TEACHES US ABOUT SHAPING CREATIVE LEADERSHIP

JAMES HAYWOOD ROLLING, JR.

palgrave
macmillan

SWARM INTELLIGENCE
Copyright © James Haywood Rolling, Jr., 2013.

First published in 2013 by PALGRAVE MACMILLAN® in the United
States—a division of St. Martin's Press LLC, 175 Fifth Avenue,
New York, NY 10010.

Where this book is distributed in the UK, Europe and the rest of the world,
this is by Palgrave Macmillan, a division of Macmillan Publishers Limited,
registered in England, company number 785998, of Houndmills,
Basingstoke, Hampshire RG21 6XS.

Palgrave Macmillan is the global academic imprint of the above companies
and has companies and representatives throughout the world.

Palgrave® and Macmillan® are registered trademarks in the United States,
the United Kingdom, Europe and other countries.

ISBN: 978-1-137-27847-0

Library of Congress Cataloging-in-Publication Data

Rolling, James Haywood, 1963–
    Swarm intelligence : what nature teaches us about shaping
creative leadership / by James Haywood Rolling, Jr.
        pages cm
      1. Creative thinking. 2. Creative ability in business. 3. Creative ability.
    4. Diffusion of innovations. 5. Swarm intelligence—Social aspects.
    I. Title.

HD53.R65 2013
658.4'092—dc23   2013017567

A catalogue record of the book is available from the British Library.

Design by Newgen Knowledge Works (P) Ltd., Chennai, India.

First edition: November 2013

10 9 8 7 6 5 4 3 2 1

Printed in the United States of America.

CONTENTS

INTRODUCTION

ANCIENT SECRET SOCIETIES AND SNOOPY'S DOGHOUSE

How do we begin to understand creativity? While all good research originates with a research question, the most relevant and enduring research almost always commences with a question that offers the most mutually advantageous result. When psychologist E. Paul Torrance started researching creativity in the 1940s, he centered on the very same query that most books on the subject focus on even today: "What is creativity?" As important as that question is, it will not be the primary focus of this book. Seeking its answer brings to mind climbing a fine and sturdy ladder raised against the wrong wall. In other words, researchers trying to describe creativity usually start by looking for it in the divergent ideas and synthesizing actions of imaginative individuals rather than where they should: earlier, at its points of social origin.

SHOW-AND-TELL

I stood in a college classroom for the first time when I was just beginning elementary school in the 1960s. I was essentially a "show-and-tell" display for my older cousin David, who wanted to refute an argument leveled during a "nature vs. nurture" debate in one of his classes at Long Island University. The general classroom discussion was nearing the conclusion that a young-ster growing up like I did, in a lower-income and predominantly African American neighborhood in Brooklyn, was highly unlikely to show a potential for creativity and individual achievement equal to that of a child growing up in an educationally nurturing, middle class environment. My cousin David, on the contrary, did not share this conclusion and to demonstrate the reason for his disagreement, he asked me to bring in my artwork and the imagi-native stories that accompanied them, so I could talk about my ideas with his classmates.

I was too young at the time to recall now if David changed any minds that day, but I vividly remember his classmates prompting me with question after question and the strange sense that they had never had a close encounter before with a boy who looked and talked like me. I enjoyed their attention. However, today I would argue that David's class was exploring the wrong question altogether. Then, as today, the "nature vs. nurture" debate sought to define creativity as either some measurable quotient of intelli-gence naturally embedded into the fabric of an individual's brain from birth, or else woven into that brain by the skilled hands of nurturing and resourceful teachers and caregivers. Thus, the ques-tion being asked by those Long Island University students was: "What is creative intelligence and how is it cultivated?" Creativity was viewed as either the product of a fortunate genetic inheritance, or of skilled and specialized instruction.

But an end-product conception of creativity immediately poses a significant problem when faced with the fact that creativity still cannot be definitively defined or measured. E. Paul Torrance is known as the "father of creativity" because he developed the Torrance Tests of Creative Thinking (TTCT), similar to IQ tests, which originally involved simple tests for evidence of divergent thinking and other problem-solving skills. In my interpretation, the premise of these tests is threefold: if we are to understand and encourage creativity, we must first be able to define it as having characteristics or qualities that are universally recognizable or meaningful in all contexts. Secondly, we must test and discover how much creativity is stored up and at work in a given brain at the time of the testing. Finally, we must analyze how the components of creativity came to be installed in that brain and measure what that individual's level of creativity enables him or her to do. Yet in a November 2012 posting on Public Radio International, James H. Borland—an expert on giftedness and a professor at Teachers College, Columbia University—reflected upon a fundamental problem: simply, there is no agreement on what creativity is. "I'm not sure I have a definition of creativity," he said. "It's one of those human constructions that isn't discovered but invented....It's a word we use in everyday speech and it makes perfect sense, but when you start to study it and try to separate out its constituent parts, it becomes more and more and more confusing."[1]

In reality, there is no specialized creativity cortex within the brain. In fact, creativity has been described as "a whole-brain activity...engaging all aspects of your brain."[2] Borland sagely goes on to point out that in the absence of agreement on what creativity is, it becomes virtually impossible to accurately measure it. Rather than seeking to understand creativity as a genetic or cultivated end product, this book will identify several systems of social interaction that are argued to be the origins of creative processes in humans and animals alike. While these processes vary, the outcomes are always the same for each involved in the process: growth and development.

IN THE ABSENCE OF AGREEMENT ON WHAT creativity is, it cannot be reduced to a particular set of individual problem-solving skills. Like language, creativity is more than its vocabulary and content—it is a behavior. Furthermore, it is much too social a behavior to be confined solely within an individual's brain. And just as there is no universal tongue that all regions and populations of the world speak as one, creativity cannot be defined as a kind of singular ability that a small percentage of us are either born with or hand-picked to excel at based on some obscure test results identifying a few of us as uniquely "gifted" in someone else's eyes. Likewise, we cannot simply assume that the majority of the human population is creatively illiterate and doomed to a life in awe of and dependent upon the talented minority. There is much more going on, much more that is possible.

Here is an analogy. Some define art as *a system of production* for creating a stock of beautiful objects and forms, requiring a formulaic mastery over the technical skills necessary to shape and present them. This is like the ceramist who crafts a delicate porcelain vase and calls it art.

Some define art as *a system of communication*, the symbolic expression of situated knowledge about a person's experience within their cultural world. Like the singer/songwriter who pens and performs a chart-topping lyric based upon the desperate experience of life growing up in a rustbelt town and calls it art.

Some define art as *a system of interrogation*, a critical-activist emancipatory practice revealing the assumptions, values, and norms that help maintain the status quo, offering a critique of unjust social relations, and empowering marginalized individuals and communities. Like the Oscar-nominated documentary filmmaker who produces a short film asking the hard questions about a failure of moral vision in society and calls it art.

Some define art as *a system of improvisation*, a practice allowing for ad hoc combinations of formulaic, symbolic, and/or critical-activist aesthetic approaches. Like the author who publishes a book of influential poems and calls it art.

Each of these definitions of creative practice readily coexists. They are in no way mutually exclusive. But the way one defines art radically changes the practical applications of creative outcomes as well as the perceived identity of an arts practitioner—artist as shaper of beauty, or artist as preserver and expresser of potent tales, or artist as shatterer of beliefs and expectations, or artist as conjurer of unimagined magic. Definitions matter. The same is the case for creativity—it will look and behave differently depending upon who and what is perceived to be creative.

But not only are there differing definitions of what some will recognize as "creative activity," there are also many differing methods for producing thought-provoking outcomes within any creative system. Take the fine arts, for example. The creative approach by which Edvard Munch organized information in 1893 about human suffering in paint on a canvas in *The Scream* was different than the creative methodology Käthe Kollwitz employed for organizing similar information in her drawings and etchings of *Woman with Dead Child* circa 1903, and different again from Alvin Ailey's methodology for organizing such information about human suffering through his 1960 choreographed dance epic surveying the African American experience in *Revelations*. These particular works of art all tell of suffering *differently*, and yet each evokes equivalent emotional authenticity about a condition that every human being will experience. Simply, there is no mathematical score on an individual achievement test that can meaningfully encompass the creativity of each of these artists or credibly suggest that because one individual's score is higher than the others, that artist wins the prize as the most creative of the bunch.

In this book I will advance the premise that the reason creativity cannot be defined as absolutely this or that is because it originates as a social behavior, not an individual one. The mythology surrounding creativity is powerful. We easily think of *his* creativity or *her* creativity, but rarely do we think of *our* creativity. Or to put it another way, creative activity and outcomes are as socially and contextually situated as they are relative to one's personal experience and resources. The social nature of creativity makes it impossible to say that one culture is more creative than another culture; at best, we can say cultures are *differently* creative. Likewise, individuals are all capable of being differently creative—a successful artist is no more or less creative than a successful scientist.

In other words, whether writers pen words, filmmakers shoot movies, singers string notes, or children swirl crayons, all creativity involves the process of making something meaningful, useful, or personally valuable from the materials at hand and with the tools we have access to. Consider the implications. If creativity originates as a social behavior, its outcomes are immediately amplified when we share our ideas, materials, and tools in schools, in the workplace, or on our own time. If creativity originates as a social behavior, everything changes with regard to the value of fostering creativity both in our selves and those we love. Nothing could be more important. Because if creativity originates as a social behavior, our creative activity is both the continuing evidence and the continuing means for the success of every individual, every family, every classroom, every society, every company, and every nation.

From a sacred perspective, one of the highest achievements of humanity is *to be fruitful and multiply*.[3] However, I believe that fruitfulness and the multiplying of human creation refers to far more than biological reproduction. What separates human beings from all other living species is the exceptionally high degree of our problem solving and tool-making acuity. Our drive and ability to converge upon the most beautiful solution, to communicate the most meaningful transmissions, to critically churn up the most advantageous questions, and to self-reflect on the possibilities of our living is unmatched in its ability to replenish our social structures.

If our ability to solve problems and make tools has been our greatest fruit, then perhaps the greatest tool for multiplying the effects of these varying behaviors has been our headlong plunges into the creative activity of those who have gone before us and whom we walk beside. Bearing fruit does not just mean giving birth to healthy offspring; it also means giddily churning our way through processes that generate an enduring array of good ideas and positive cumulative benefits for those who will follow behind us. Bearing fruit means leaving behind a stir of echoes that broadcasts the character and content of our collective and individual achievements for generations after we have walked this earth.

Creativity is a collective force that reinforces the success of the human species across innumerable fronts; creative activity is akin to entering a great energy flow that—like "The Force" described in the series of *Star Wars* films—surrounds us, penetrates us, and binds us together with others who share the same mental materials and tools. All that creativity requires is proximity to others. *Creativity is, literally, human development in action.* However, the proximity necessary to ensure mutual social development may come through unexpected routes that don't actually require being in the physical vicinity of those one is behaving with. It is clear that the complexity of this topic returns us to the issue of what questions will best guide our journey to more fully understand creativity.

I will not begin by asking, "What is creativity?" Instead, I will unravel two simultaneous questions that will best support this book's advocacy for innovation and creativity in business and education alike. First, I ask: "Where is creativity located?" Secondly, I ask: "Why does creativity matter?"

STARTING ELSEWHERE

When I was a child, I discovered I was a part of an ancient secret society, a society of individuals who drew pictures of the worlds unfolding within their imagination; I learned how to read the society's creative codes and recode them as my own. I discovered my affiliation with this society while mining deep into the black plastic bags in my father's closet, filled with Marvel and DC comics featuring superheroes and tales from the crypt. I introduced myself to other kinds of visual and written codes as I paged through anthologies on my father's art studio bookshelves by artists ranging from Charles Schulz, the creator of *Peanuts*, to the dark worlds of Charles Addams, to the obscure illustrators of risqué pulp advertisements and girlie drawings of repressed 1950s and countercultural 1960s Americana.

By learning to decode the shifting and intersecting patterns of words, images, ambiguity, and double entendres, I also became fluent in my communication of the code. I was encountering countless artists engaged in rendering experience and imagination through pictures on paper, and I flowed into the seams between those images at every opportunity to steal a look. My father—a professional artist in a post–Civil Rights era when most African American men raising families sought secure jobs as public employees—was a bold man and a stubborn man, but he wasn't a very sharing man. I had to sneak into my father's studio to enjoy this treasure trove, always taking care to put every book back exactly as I found it or risk his anger.

Nevertheless, my father and I did share membership in this secret society. We became fellow citizens moving in a parallel trajectory, makers of new visual patterns along the way. Like all these other artists I encountered, my ambition became to make marks that came to life as stories. And in these visual stories, as within the inner labyrinths of Snoopy's doghouse that always seemed packed with miles of subterranean storage vaults and corridors, I initiated connections to other selves—unexpected possibilities, and imagined worlds—sharing them with anyone who was interested in the narratives of space battles and underground cities I penciled into being on each page of the large bond paper layout pads my father gave to me.

Where is creativity located? Creativity is not locked within; we first encounter creativity in enticing patterns of behavior that exist outside of ourselves and to which we are compelled to grasp. The location of the most enticing creative activity is always just beyond your self—which, like the carrot dangled before the horse, provides the impetus for us to move forward, connect, and multiply our interactions with other society members.

BUILDING A BETTER MOUSETRAP

Thomas Edison did not invent the incandescent light bulb. That idea preceded Edison by at least 50 years. In fact, Edison's most productive innovation was arguably the creation of experimental facilities and the assembly of a creative leadership team established in Menlo Park, New Jersey, in 1876. In the six-year burst of creative activity that followed immediately thereafter, Edison patented approximately 400 inventions, including the phonograph, numerous devices for producing electric light, and important components to a test model for generating and transmitting power featuring a centrally located supply of energy. Edison, also known as the "Wizard of Menlo Park," intended for new users of electrical energy to tap into the central power source through a system of pipes modeled after the very first successful long distance natural gas pipeline in the United States, an underground structure that was completed in Pennsylvania in 1872 just a few years prior to the establishment of the Menlo Park laboratory facilities. A few sentences of handwritten notes by Edison dated somewhere around 1880 in a prospectus referring specifically to "Electricity vs. Gas as General Illuminants" serves to outline the following business objective:

> Object, Edison to effect exact imitation of all done by gas, so as to replace lighting by gas, by lighting by electricity. To improve the illumination to such an extent as to meet all requirements of natural, artificial, and commercial conditions.[4]

Most importantly to our story, Edison's Menlo Park laboratory was also a business model capable of improving upon the idea of the incandescent light bulb while garnering significant capital investment to do so largely by building a "better mousetrap."[5] When Edison incorporated the Electric Light Co. in November of 1878, its mission was simple and destined to be profoundly effective—the Menlo Park research and development team sought only to imitate the patterns of successful models of technology (gas and water utilities, telegraphy, and arc lighting) that had already been accepted as a schema of urban development within the public and corporate consciousness.

Edison recognized that this familiarity "provided the public with the means for quickly understanding the value of his new system and how to interact with it."[6] The collective creative force of the Menlo Park team during this six-year period is perhaps best exemplified in a notation that Thomas Edison was so in sync within this hive of activity that "it is difficult to distinguish his actions from those of his colleagues."[7] Francis Jehl, one of his long-time assistants, divulged the point of fact that "Edison is in reality a collective noun and refers to the work of many men."[8]

SINCE THE EARLY GRADES OF ELEMENTARY SCHOOL, I was identified and tracked as gifted and talented, the best evidence of which was usually my self-initiated creative activities. But reflecting on this fact also compels me to radically rethink some notions of creative giftedness and talent. The collective creation of culture requires that "from one generation to the next, via teaching and imitation…knowledge, values, and other factors that influence behavior" must be transmitted.[9] According to the influential twentieth-century cognitive developmental theory of Lev Semenovich Vygotsky, the brain is wired to learn from the sociocultural influences that surround it; individual cognitive development begins with myriad independent internalizations of what was once elsewhere in proximity.[10] The social origins of such transmissions have huge implications for individual learning and an accurate understanding of creativity in action.

A culture is a complex pattern of human behaviors, systemized to sustain both itself and the multiple agents that perpetuate it. Through independent and decentralized choices, these agents—or cultural workers—somehow coalesce meaning from the chaos of life and purposefully render that meaning into coherent and recognizable patterns through mark-making, representative models, and aesthetic interventions. In this way, our works of art—written, visual, and performed—all serve as biocultural mechanisms transmitting and then initiating every social pattern that matters most.

But isolated agents cannot in themselves constitute cultural patterns; others must be enticed to do likewise. Culture requires that individuals be enticed to adopt the same patterns of behavior as those that preceded them—this works like the excreted or secreted attractors in ant colonies, chemical pheromones triggering a likewise response in the members of their community so that the next insects along the way will follow the very same scent trail to a new food source.[11] Not surprisingly, the complexity of human behavior requires a much more cerebral kind of enticement. Utilizing a term first coined by Charles J. Lumsden and E. O. Wilson, such enticements may be called "culturgens," described as "genes" that operate in the social body rather than individual human bodies.[12] The potential to augment one's gene pool with successful behaviors can be overwhelmingly attractive, and just as assuredly, these "culturgens" will also attract others. They are passed directly from mind to mind, selected for mutually beneficial coevolutionary advantages that will preserve the resilience of a diverse social group—such as the common sympathetic response to an infant's needful cry, or the incest taboo shared by all societies, or audiences worldwide finding humor and pathos in the same traveling exhibition of paintings and prints, or the avid response of a nation to a best-selling new book revealing a story too long invisible.

As such, these enticements do more to cultivate individual talent and creativity than we realize, always stemming from the transmissions of a swarm of other thinkers and doers.[13] And similarly as throughout the natural world, these socially situated enticements are ideal for either maintaining the direction or rapidly altering the development of the human behavioral patterns. In a thriving culture, just like in a relay race, the self-initiated creative activities of individuals are originated elsewhere until the next creative mind grabs the baton and runs with it. In other words, my "giftedness" was gifted to me from countless others and will be passed along in turn.

Why does creativity matter? Edison understood that creativity is a means for ensuring the successful perpetuation of patterns that sustain our lives. His system of lighting was intended to displace other established systems for energy and illumination only in as much as it was "a better mousetrap" and would in turn become an enticement for the development of successive technologies. In other words, the purpose of creativity is to replicate and proliferate successful patterns for living.

A CALL TO ADVENTURE

A recent *Newsweek* cover article entitled "The Creativity Crisis" provided a dire statistic: Since 1990, scores measuring creativity among American children have been steadily decreasing.[14] Without an agreed-upon definition of creativity, it is admittedly difficult to verify this assertion of declining creative achievement. It is far more useful in the effort to corroborate the existence of a crisis to ask the question, "Where is creativity located?" The obvious answer is: not in the center of schooling expectations. The focus on high-stakes testing and standardized curricula in our public schools is stifling collaborative creative engagement among students, and students are responding by tuning out.

Studies have long revealed how learning disengagement leads to patterns of chronic absenteeism, cutting class, course failure, and high dropout rates. Although concentrated in what we commonly term "failing schools," this disengagement can be found in every city of America, and in every school district. Approximately 1.3 million students fail to graduate from high school every year, and even after over a decade of increased attention and some improvement, the number is once again on the rise. Altogether, as many as a quarter of our students aren't finishing high school. Not only are we not expecting creativity from youngsters, we aren't expecting creativity from teachers either. Where is creativity?

According to many studies, a leading indicator of disengaged learning is a regimented educational environment that stymies creativity—leaving children cut off from inclinations they are naturally born to pursue and boxed into sequentially arranged learning contexts where creativity does not matter much at all.

In an online brief titled "At-Risk Youth and the Creative Process," Linda Kreger Silverman wrote that, "the school curriculum is sequential, the textbooks are sequential, the workbooks are sequential, the teaching methods are sequential, and most teachers learn sequentially."[15] Children are graded on their mastery of sequential subjects, but not on the mastery of the creative things they love to do over and over again, thereby reinforcing their own understandings. Children are brilliant non-linear learners, identifying useful patterns out of the chaos of stimuli that arises from even the simplest and most random exposures to the world and mimicking those patterns through repetition. This is how children first learn to speak a language.

Non-linear adaptive mimicry is the natural quality of learning that emerges from spontaneous human connections and communication. Similar to the way human memory works, this non-linear interactivity is evident in the back-and-forth dialogues between parent and child, or between child and sibling or playmate. On a recent family visit just before Labor Day in 2011, my wife and I took my youngest brother and his family to a local park near our home in the Central New York region. While we were there, I watched my three nieces involve themselves in a self-initiated civil engineering project at a small section of Mill Creek in Syracuse, diverting the flow of water into mini-rapids and micro-pools. It may have been play but they worked hard at it, prodding each other along with new suggestions about which stones along the streambed to move or shift or stack for close to an hour, each attempting to mimic the prior attempt. Whether it is three children or a culture of three million, the same can be said: *Creativity is a common, collective, self-organizing, adaptive, non-linear social networking behavior.*

The consequence of forcing non-linear and dynamic mental processes into narrow channels of schooled expectations is the severed engagement of far too many learners. Not surprising. Children can be seriously injured when sent out to play in "railroad yards"—that is to say, herded one by one through a model of education based on sequences and schedules that has persisted since the Industrial Revolution. What is the worst consequence of this disengagement from learning? According to a recent study, over time, chronically disengaged and uninterested learners often manifest psychological distress, mood and anxiety disorders, gravitate toward the diverting risks of substance use, and display the onset of antisocial behaviors as teenagers.[16] While some disengaged learners may find a pathway to success, most disengaged learners lose touch with the creativity that surrounds them.

"Where is creativity?" has also become a driving question in the global economy as inventiveness and innovation are increasingly recognized as vital to success in the twenty-first-century job market.[17] A recent IBM survey found that 1,500 CEOs in 60 countries identified creativity as the number one leadership quality of the future. Nationally, studies have shown that employers place increasing value on applied skills such as problem solving, collaboration, and creativity as crucial for the success and improvement of the contemporary workforce.[18] U.S. employers rate creativity and innovation among the top five skills and rank arts study as one of the most important indicators of a potential creative worker.[19]

The New Commission on the Skills of the American Workforce urgently calls for rethinking schooling practices and public education policies so that America does not permanently lose its pre-eminence in the global economy.[20] Professional graduate school programs are also increasingly recognizing the role of the arts in developing advanced workforce skills. At least forty MBA programs now feature design courses, which are valued for the way they combine aesthetics with environmental responsibility, experimental skill in manipulating symbols, sounds, and materials, and an understanding of consumer preference and commercial needs.[21]

But relocating creativity to the center of the conversation in business and education will not be enough unless we also radically think the question, "Why does creativity matter?" America is at risk of falling hopelessly behind unless extreme steps are taken to address the creativity crisis that is looming, if not already here. In every chapter of *Swarm Intelligence*, I will argue the reason as to why we need to turn our classrooms into crucibles for collective, collaborative, swarming creativity. Employing an accessible and narrative approach to cutting-edge research at the intersection of biological swarm theory, systems theory, and complexity theory, *Swarm Intelligence* will show that the pursuit of collective creativity is the fundamental basis for attaining our greatest potential as learners, as a nation too often divided, and as a member of a global network of vastly differing cultures and social agendas. Individual achievement is a pleasant byproduct of collaborative social interaction and culture building.

THIS BOOK PRESENTS THE LATEST SWARM THEORY research and is structured to show how it is directly relevant to the way human social behavior manifests creativity. I will show how humans achieve more while working and playing in concert than we can as rugged individualists, and that individual creative achievement originates from our natural behavior as social beings. This book will also draw on contemporary systems theory, emphasizing how our cultural systems are always more than the sum of the parts any individual members may contribute. Further, a brief exploration of complexity theory will demonstrate that complex creative behavior emerges from a few simple rules, and that all cultural systems are networks of many interdependent individuals who interact according to those rules. *Swarm Intelligence* will show that teaching creativity is much more than a task of preparing selected students to be excellent artists—teaching creativity is the vital ingredient to preparing smarter, fully engaged problem solvers with the tools necessary for success in the twenty-first century.

Swarm Intelligence will ultimately show how congregating into social networks in and out of classrooms makes us *all* smarter. Human beings possess the unique ability to create metaphors of what our minds are doing at any given time—casting our ideas and understandings out into the world through marks and schematics on a page or canvas, physical objects and mathematical models, and evocative performances so that others might also understand. This is how individual creativity entices others toward the construction of a common culture. We naturally coalesce into our own creative communities—hives for the growth of our particular swarm of thinkers and doers. I will argue that schools must aid this process, not impede it.

Ultimately, I will also present several solutions for cultivating a creative, collaborative and curious twenty-first-century work force.[22] *Swarm Intelligence* is offered as an argument against the diminishment of creativity that occurs incrementally through overly regimented schooling and workplace practices, and as a remedy to the powerful mythology that some people are gifted with special creative capacities while most others are not. Toward these aims, *Swarm Intelligence* explores six crucial areas of human interaction through which individual creativity can be collectively fostered: social networks, systems, swarms, superorganisms, stories, and schools. This book introduces readers to the symbiotic relationship between collective creativity and individual creativity through a decidedly autobiographical lens, as well as through many other relevant stories and models of socially based creative growth and development.

Swarm Intelligence begins by introducing the undervalued and misunderstood nature of individual creativity and the misdirection of efforts to define and delimit it as either a set of learned skills or an intellectual gift from the heavens. I also preface the ensuing adventure with recent research and commissioned reports documenting a growing lack of creativity in the arena of public education. *Swarm Intelligence* will next challenge each reader to rethink what they believe they know about creativity in a chapter on how creativity is *underdeveloped*, comprised of insights drawn from popular culture, personal anecdotes, and the persistence of twentieth century behaviorist approaches to educational policy and workplace management still practiced today.

Swarm Intelligence will go on to reveal and rethink social networks as a crucial arena of interpersonal interaction and creativity that will aid the reader's personal growth and the transformation of their social contexts. I retell the story of the significance of Facebook, Google, and YouTube from the perspective of the self-organizing social network of disaffected young people that spilled out into the streets during Egypt's 18-Day Revolution; I also recount the developmental importance of the collaborative creative play we first became familiar with around the time we entered kindergarten.

This book will also explore the development of generative systems of human social behavior as a crucial arena of collective intelligence and creativity. *Swarm Intelligence* will provide a simple explanation of systems theory concepts along with examples of creative social behavior, such as the birth of American jazz to the evolution from agrarian to agricultural to mercantile economic systems. These are examples of complex systems of group interaction that have changed the trajectory of contemporary culture, as well as the identities of countless individuals. Subsequent chapters respectively explore biological and zoological swarms, mutually benefitting organisms behaving together as superorganisms, and experiential stories occupying the consciousness as models to live by—each in and of itself providing an interactive arena for building and sustaining collaborative leadership and creativity.

One of my doctoral students, David Rufo, works with his teaching partner Greg Sommer as fourth grade classroom teachers at the Manlius Pebble Hill School near Syracuse, New York. In 2012, we co-presented at the National Art Education Association convention in New York City on a theory of creativity David describes in this way:

Early in the 2010–2011 school year I noticed that the students in my fourth-grade classroom did their best creative work when allowed student agency and choice in a child-centered learning environment often resulting in an energized, cooperative working paradigm we came to refer to as the bUzZ. During the spring semester I decided to engage in an action research project in order to see if I could ascertain the classroom characteristics that lead to a bUzZ and how it might be sustained once underway. I found that the bUzZ closely resembled swarm dynamics found in nature which led me to a whole new understanding of education, how students function within a classroom space, and what it means to be a teacher.

In an effort to more fully describe the "swarm dynamics" these two teachers have fostered in their classroom, I offer a chapter emphasizing the need to reinvent schools as the crucible of a more moral approach to public education. Moreover, the buzz of creative activity described as being so evident in David and Greg's classroom also suggests a more *productive* approach to public education. My examination of promising theory and practices for fostering greater collective achievement will also provide some concrete suggestions for aiding students in the development of their fullest potential as contributing members of society and as creative individuals.

Lastly, I will conclude with a chapter rethinking creativity as the natural byproduct of swarm intelligence and suggesting a living curriculum for learners and workers seeking to cultivate enduring habits of innovation.

The stakes are high. In a recently released report by the President's Committee on the Arts and the Humanities titled *Reinvesting in Arts Education: Winning America's Future through Creative Schools,* the crisis of creativity in our nation today is addressed from the point of view of K-12 public school education in the United States. In it, a key proposition from President

Obama's 2011 State of the Union Address is transmitted in the form of a challenge as to "whether all of us—as citizens, and as parents—are willing to do what's necessary to give every child a chance to succeed."[23]

In response to this call for action, how are we prepared to behave? Where do we go from here?

CHAPTER ONE

HOW TO UNDERDEVELOP CREATIVITY

Tom Kelley—the general manager of IDEO, a cutting-edge international design firm and innovation consultant—gave a talk several years ago where he recounted a story told by artist and Hallmark card designer Gordon MacKenzie, at the beginning of MacKenzie's book *Orbiting the Giant Hairball*.[1] As a fellow designer, the story was important enough to Kelley to recount in his own talk: it was ultimately about how to underdevelop creativity. MacKenzie had been asked to give a demonstration of his sculpture practice at a K-6 grade school where his wife served as a cultural arts coordinator, and he was scheduled one morning to meet one grade level at a time for 50 minutes each.

MacKenzie started his conversation with each group by identifying himself as an artist who loved hanging out with other creative human beings, and asked the very same curious question: how many other artists there were in the room? In the kindergarten group, every child enthusiastically raised his or her hand, and sometimes two hands. Every first grader raised a hand as well. But in each grade after that there was more uncertainty and attrition so that by the time MacKenzie asked the sixth graders his question, he was compelled to wonder out loud whether all the creative people had transferred to another school. Only one or two sixth graders identified themselves as artists—and their hands were raised timidly at best.

MacKenzie's revelation is that one of the best places to under-develop creativity is in schools charged with the responsibility of aiding the development of learning. Andrew Grant and Gaia Grant replicated evidence of the steady attrition of creative identity over the course of a youngster's K-12 education in their own experiment.[2] These two educators visited schools wondering if contemporary schooling kills creativity over time. In order to find out, they surveyed classes from grade to grade asking, "Who thinks they are creative?," "Who's good at making things and building things and designing things?," "Who's a good artist?" In preschool, fourteen out of fourteen hands went up. In kindergarten, the affirmative response was ten out of ten. By sixth grade, the response was ten out of eighteen hands up. By eleventh grade, only one youngster identified himself as creative.

So what are students today learning that so stifles the development of personal creative identity? Actually, this is the wrong question. The problem isn't *what* youngsters are learning, it's *how* they are learning it.

Some of the most creative minds in the world have been the products of a public school education. I myself am proud to say I am the product of this system, but I had influences and opportunities outside of school that made me the artist I am today. I don't even remember my in-school art education in elementary and middle school; in fact, my creative, daydreaming character-istics were often deemed a distraction to the real schoolwork at hand. There is something that goes on daily in schools throughout the world that de-emphasizes the importance of creativity. And as Gordon MacKenzie and the Grants found out firsthand, whatever is going on has been extremely successful at doing so.

Arguing that the current system of public education produces a number of creative individuals misses the point if we do not also acknowledge the profound numbers of students who graduate believing they are not creative. How many innovators, inventors, and transformational thinkers have already been lost to us in the process of getting their education? How many new ideas have been dumbed down or stillborn in the hearts of friends and neighbors and loved ones who have no confidence in themselves as creative beings? And if the primary goal of public education in the United States is not to develop the creative capacity of each student, what has been the de facto reason for sending kids to school? To answer these questions, one has to go back to an earlier time, as pub-lic education was finally becoming a mandatory experience for youngsters throughout the nation in the twentieth century.

THE RISE OF EARLY TWENTIETH CENTURY BEHAVIORISM, with its core belief that all human and animal behavior could be condi-tioned to perform optimally through the proper scientific tech-niques, coincided with a point in history when every state finally had compulsory schooling laws on the books mandating that all children complete elementary school. This was an unfortunate coincidence since the great flaw of behaviorism was its reduction of the complexities of human development to cause and effect mechanics.

Within institutions that adopted a behaviorist approach to education and training, the learned responses of human beings were attributed to the carefully controlled introduction of selected stimuli—essentially, an ongoing experiment in the manipulation of human behavior by their teachers and instructors. In retrospect this was not only simplistic, it was unethical. Most students and parents would never assent to the idea that the results of classroom assignments or exams should determine the tracking of schooling opportunities or career choices for the rest of a student's life, yet such decisions by educators were often the norm. Behaviorism's influence reached its height just in time to converge with a scientific fervor to identify the most modern means for providing a free education to the general public; therefore it shouldn't be surprising that the principles of behaviorism still affect the way schools work today.

In 1908, Charles W. Eliot, the president of Harvard University, expressed a very commonly held belief in the efficacy of this approach. When he was questioned how best to decide which children should go to industrial schools, which to ordinary high schools, and which to mechanics art high schools, Eliot's response was that schoolteachers "ought to sort the pupils and sort them by their evident and probable destinies."[3] In Eliot's learned opinion, such controlled experiments on the direction of the lives of young learners were the day-to-day management responsibility of their teachers and school administrators.

Behaviorist theories tended to oversimplify teaching and learning, which were seen as little more than a cause-and-effect conditioning exercise with students akin to Pavlov's dogs, animals whose behavior was controlled and directed through a famous series of experiments involving extrinsic motivations (i.e., rewards vs. punishments) in ways that were easily replicable. The historical evidence that behaviorist approaches were also applied to humans is not difficult to find—for instance, most of us today are unaware that Pavlov later conducted his experiments on children as well. During the heyday of the Child-study movement in the late 1800s and early 1900s, which was "the first organized movement to target public school reform in the United States,"[4] scientific beliefs about the development of humans suggested that youngsters grew in stages similar to all other biological organisms. Others, besides Pavlov, sought to put this "science" to the test.

Unfortunately, the excitement of discovery and new potential often has a way of escalating basic beliefs into unabated and almost religious fervor—even if they are scientific beliefs. The enthusiasm for science as the answer to all of society's ills[5] ultimately led to the infiltration of pseudo-sciences like craniology, phrenology, and physiognomy into public schooling, each of which "assumed that the measurement of attributes like head size, jaw angle, and limb length inferred human character and potential."[6] Because of its overt similarities, this cult of measurement easily took root alongside behaviorism, entwining the demand for quantification with the belief that the true nature of objects must be classified solely through the power of scientific observation, testing, and evaluation. Consequently, these beliefs also got hopelessly tangled together into the extreme notion that visual bodily markers and numerical scores—in their conformity or nonconformity to prevailing norms—were the tacit predictors of what kind of adult a student would grow up to be.

Eliot and other influential American educators were convinced that teaching and learning conducted as a scientific experiment—in which a teacher makes visual observations about each student, introduces changes, and then notes their effects—ultimately offered the fullest and most efficient control over all student outcomes, including their destinies. And if your focus as an educator is on controlled student outcomes, the last thing you are interested in is the development of divergent thinking in learners. This is one of the better ways to underdevelop creativity.

AROUND THE SAME TIME THAT BEHAVIORISM and the controlled observation of children were being embraced by American educators, Frederick Winslow Taylor was carefully scrutinizing occupational practices in paper mills as well as during the factory production of steel. Known as the father of "scientific management," Taylor was a pioneer in the introduction of new concepts of industrial efficiency as one of the first paid management consultants to big business in the United States. It was a time—between 1900 and 1910—when the American public school system was in a state of a crisis. The improvement of U.S. child labor laws and compulsory education policies had combined with huge increases in the enrollment of "non-English-speaking children from semiliterate families," new immigrants to our shores "predominantly from the poorest socioeconomic groups in southern and eastern Europe,"[7] such that "elementary classes of over one hundred children were common."[8] This was also an inflationary period in the nation's economy with sharply rising costs of living, a shortage of tax revenue to support public institutions, and U.S. citizens increasingly wary of inefficiency and waste.

Moreover, in 1909 the public had been introduced to a book by Leonard P. Ayres titled *Laggards in Our Schools*—a survey of deplorably overcrowded, poorly managed school systems in 58 cities that failed to meet the standards of Ayres's statistically concocted "Index of Efficiency." Ayres had written a scathing indictment of the production of what he defined as "retarded" children—over-aged learners repeating the same material in their grades over and over again—and in doing so, he was "one of the first educators to picture the school as a factory"[9] that required the application of the best business and industrial practices. Hence, education reform crusaders were more than ready to embrace Taylor's new system of scientific management almost as soon as it was introduced to them.

Taylor's ideas about efficiency were first catapulted into the American consciousness after they were featured during a 1910 Capitol Hill hearing before the Interstate Commerce Commission attempting to resolve a legal wrangle between a railroad trade association, industry management, and merchants. Proposed increases in freight rates threatened to damage bottom-line profits across the board. For some of the stakeholders, the priority was to find a means of *lowering* costs; for others the priority was *increasing* wages for workers. At just the right moment, Taylor's system was suddenly thrust into the spotlight as a "magic" panacea with the potential to make management in all sectors of industry—including the management of schools—as efficient as possible, supposedly to the benefit of all stakeholders involved.

First, Taylor mandated the replacement of diverse and rule-of-thumb workplace methods with the single best, scientifically determined method for doing a task. Anything less than that system, as determined by management, was considered a waste of time and money. Laborers who collaborated to create their own ad hoc methods in the field or on the work floor were supposedly contributing to lessened productivity. When this mandate was replicated in an educational context, opportunities for learners to figure out problems without directives from their teachers were severely curtailed, further underdeveloping creativity.

Second, Taylor's system also required the scientific selection, training, and development of each employee, rather than leaving employees to train themselves. Or, as Taylor once put it to a mechanic who worked under him, common laborers were "not supposed to think" because "there are other people paid for thinking around here."[10] Taylor maintained that "one type of man is needed to plan ahead and an entirely different type to execute the work."[11] When adopted by schools, this approach led to what John D. Philbrick long ago observed as "the imposition of tasks; if the pupil likes it, well; if not, the obligation is the same."[12] The assumption that the teacher, or manager, is solely responsible for devising and planning activities and projects serves to underdevelop creativity both in learners, the professional workforce, and throughout society.

Third, Taylor's scientific management system required the provision of detailed instruction and supervision, ensuring that workers were applying all principles precisely as instructed in their performance and completion of each assigned task—so much so that the stopwatch became emblematic of Taylor's system, often likened to "management by measurement." As Taylor's approach was applied in schools, the completion of homework assignments, sequenced workbooks, and timed tests became the order of the school day. Think about it. Workbooks are essentially books of assignments and their rules—conditioning tools in which the teacher introduces changes, notes effects, and maintains full control over the design of the student. Workbooks are analogous to any and all means of social regimentation. These "conditioning books" are used in order to measure an individual's gradual acquisition and application of instructional or institutional content, but they also serve to underdevelop creativity.

Fourth, Taylor insisted upon a strict division of labor between management and workers so that managers carry the burden of "analyzing, planning, and controlling the whole manufacturing process," and each worker carries the burden of doing only what he or she is told to do.[13] Management-focused schooling models— their primary mandate being the efficient conveyance of learners from one grade to the next—also view the highest student achievers as those best conditioned to perform in accord with standardized rules, regulations, and tests. Meanwhile, in the cultivation of cadres of individual achievers that meet the prevailing standard, "creative mentalities" go underdeveloped.

Perhaps the greatest detriment regarding Taylor's system was that while it made great sense toward increasing the production of manufactured goods in factory assembly lines, when applied to schools it resulted in a focus upon increasing the production of graduating students ready to enter a managed workforce—while *decreasing* any investment in the development of creativity among those students or in their learning experiences. The fact that public schools by and large still operate this way continues to underdevelop the creativity of millions of young people.

WHAT IF NEO HAD TAKEN THE BLUE PILL? One of the underlying messages in the hugely popular 1999 sci-fi/action flick titled *The Matrix* is about how easy it is to reject the possibility that we are capable of extraordinary things in everyday life. The setting of the film is in a future wherein, from infancy, human thought is dictated and manufactured by computers, rendering human beings into docile energy sources. Living batteries. The main character, named Thomas Anderson, is also held captive by a "reality" written in cyber-language and force-fed directly into his brain—except that in his secret identity as a computer hacker named "Neo," he has been subconsciously resisting his captivity and is about to become fully aware of his circumstances for the very first time.

Early in the movie Anderson is contacted over a cell phone by a mysterious character named Morpheus who knows all about his extracurricular activities and his alternate identity. Addressed only as Neo by his new allies, our hero is confronted with the opportunity to begin a personal adventure by first evading capture and interrogation at the hands of the threatening agents who are tracking him. Morpheus advises Neo to escape through the most extreme route imaginable—tiptoeing to freedom along the very windy ledge of a very tall building. Neo instead chooses what appears to be the less risky option—allowing himself to be handcuffed and taken into custody. This is all an allegory for the many ways in which we arrest our own development before it ever truly begins.

Later, at perhaps the pivotal point in the film, our hero is again confronted with a choice—this time between a red pill and a blue pill. Consume the red pill and Neo joins a rebellion, the familiar framework of his identity catastrophically falling away as he is irrevocably expelled from his disabling containment. Consume the blue pill and Neo wakes up comfortably unintruded upon by alternative realities, firmly wedged once again into the cradle of his familiar world. Neo opts this time to topple the framework of his arrested development: no longer refusing the call to adventure, Neo embarks on a quest to hack his way out of his limitations and finally become himself.

Our hero's identity is changed the moment he is ejected from his claustrophobic containment.

Near the film's conclusion when Neo is mortally wounded, he finally allows the stubborn perception of his flesh and blood limitations to succumb and is suddenly freed from his psychological self-limitations, or containments, as well. Resurrected, all faculties unfettered, he is for the first time able to fully perceive "the Matrix," the programming code that constitutes all identifiers and underlies all creative potential. At that instant, all of Neo's boundaries become immaterial, all identities immediately inhabitable, all possibilities available. Neo becomes fluid and fully awake, the mobility of his self-concept unbounded. In one memorable scene, it becomes evident to our hero that the borders of perception may be bent aside with no more energy than it takes to draw a breath. At the very end of the film, the sky is the only limit for Neo—to be alive is to launch into adventure, to creatively network with possibilities as you soar to new heights.

If Neo symbolizes the primal human thrust to express one's creativity, how, in contrast, does creativity so easily become underdeveloped? How do we find ourselves locked into unnecessary containments, shielded from our greatest potential? Why do so many of us take the easy path and reject the call to adventure without a second thought? A useful clue as to where adventure is typically forestalled is readily found by taking a second look at Neo's identity at the start of the film—when he is still living a secret life as a hacker, illegally accessing networks of information and resources to gain unauthorized access to the data he needs and desires.

In other words, Neo's creativity is first framed as a criminal offense, a transgression against social standards and expectations.

His creativity is a danger to the status quo; it is why the suit-clad agents Neo initially fears are looking for him in the first place. The knack that Neo had somehow developed for escaping the numbing routines of his daily existence each night—hacking through institutional firewalls intended both to thwart and contain him—also began attracting the attention of friends and foes alike. Creativity is destabilizing, but it is also incredibly enticing. It excavates the undiscovered resources embedded in the social landscape and shifts a society's center of gravity in preparation for an advance that is mutually advantageous to all. Yet unlike Neo, most of us continue to live our lives more thwarted and contained than we care to admit.

WE ARE LIVING IN A DIGITAL AGE that demands creativity, entrepreneurship and nimble, adaptable new product innovations. Yet, another way to underdevelop creativity is by burying it in layers of misperception, rendering it as invisible. In a recent *New York Times* Op-Ed piece, David Brooks cited "a smart question" posed by cognitive scientist Steven Pinker, one that served as the premise for Brooks' written reflection on what he titled the "Tools of Thinking." According to Brooks, Pinker asked: "What scientific concept would improve everybody's cognitive toolkit?" For example, a long time ago, most people on the planet assumed the earth was the center of the universe and that assumption made us very locally bound, insulated, and frightened about what we didn't know. Afraid about falling over the edge of our feared limitations, most societies played it safe, displaying a piously justified lack of inquiry. Exploration was dangerous, let alone the likelihood of being placed on trial for suspicion of heresy. Nevertheless, the scientific revolution championed by Copernicus and later by Galileo did more than shift our focal point from the earth to the sun and beyond. Cognitively, it opened our eyes to the radical power of simple and disciplined observation.

Pinker was suggesting that there is some next great twenty-first-century scientific revolution on the horizon waiting to happen to us all. But the idea that there is a key scientific concept missing from some of our toolkits lends to a misperception, causing us to rush right past a vital understanding. It is indeed true that the history of human intellectual achievement is a shared toolkit of preserved and applied knowledge that has made us smarter than every other living being on the planet. However, of all our collected tools, scientific methods are not that old.

Unfortunately, our scientific achievements have done an excellent job of almost entirely obscuring the crucial relevance of the arts to human social development. The history of human civilization reveals that aesthetically shaped avenues for critical thinking, information recall, the cultivation of new learning, and making carefully reasoned choices regarding the human condition long *preceded* the sciences and also made us very smart along the way. In general, these cultural practices are known as the *humanities*, and have included discourses and study the areas of language, literature, history, religion, philosophy, visual arts and design, music, and theater. Several areas of the humanities have been positively augmented by scientific methods and also fitted under the category of *social sciences*, such as history, anthropology, sociology, linguistics, psychology, and political science. The point here is, what if the next great cognitive revolution waiting to happen is not scientific at all, but is better characterized as a creative transformation similar to Neo's?

The arts, design, the humanities, and storytelling are just some of the many aesthetic means for capturing, communicating, and cataloguing the things and ideas human beings find to be meaningful. Nevertheless, they are only tools for making meaning—tools that may come into favor because they are appropriate for the need at hand, yet will ultimately be replaced by other tools, better at addressing new needs as they arise in 2012 and beyond. No tool is indispensable—neither our scientific tools, nor our artistic ones. What *is* indispensable is the toolkit itself, the age-old, common, collective, self-organizing, and adaptive human behavior we call creativity.

Our creativity is a social form of intelligence, allowing us to connect, relate, join forces, and pool our resources, so that we are all less alone, less vulnerable, and less unable. We are compelled from infancy to connect with parents and caregivers, making sense of a confusing world because unless we do so, we cannot survive; then we struggle to maintain our networks as adults because as our connections are lost, we are slowly diminished. Our creativity makes us agents of change; underdeveloped or untapped creativity renders us exploitable as agents of the status quo.

Through the force of our creativity—both our arts and our sciences—we affect the surrounding world for our mutual gain. Our creativity cultivates relationships with family, friends, allies, and process as resources and tools toward making ourselves ever more effectual. It allows us to aggregate the bits of knowledge and understanding we already own along with those bits we come to share so that the dimensions of our footprints behind us reflect the full weight of our society and culture, not just our solitary frames. Our cultural achievements as a human race are always collaborative. By definition, cultural achievements are not individual achievements. A culture—or a nation—is an amalgamation of compounding collective achievements.

We follow up the ideas of those who have gone before us and move in pace with the discoveries of those alongside us; we share the mass and momentum of a mighty assembly. Creativity is creative activity that reproduces or improves upon prior successes in addressing what is needed or desired. As a result of a swarm of creative activity, the effects on our common culture are incremental but consistent: a convergence of creative practices result in culture's evolution. We move in and out of creative swarms all of our lives and the outcomes of our shared social imagination make us *all* smarter and better equipped for living.

AT A RECENT FAMILY FUNERAL, I enjoyed an extended conversation with one of my wife's cousins, Courtney, who works as a custom car care specialist and detailer. Courtney related a story about a former co-worker who did not fit in with the team responsible for the innovative approaches their clients had come to expect. Courtney explained that the former co-worker had been previously trained and employed in a local factory. In particular, he noted this ex-employee's inability to adapt and create in the field—he lacked the experience and aptitude for using or applying tools and materials in innovative and unexpected ways. This inability struck me as an example of a "workbook mentality," so often produced as the outcome of an education that does not value creativity, a mentality that has been trained to recognize only the problems that have been assigned, to address only the boxes and parameters that have been prescribed, and to believe that the only meaningful answers are those in the back of the book.

Widespread attendance of public schools became the norm after many psychologists had begun "to make use of scientific methods of observation and aggregation of data to investigate problems like [human will] in children, criminality in adults, delinquency in juveniles, and degeneracy in races."[14] The observable characteristics of the young "were thought to be speakers of the quality of an interior germ,"[15] that is to say, the physical evidence that a youngster would grow up to be either a contributing citizen or a drain upon society; likewise, the psychological development of the young was expected to be a recapitulation of what has come to be understood as an evolutionary model, based largely on the genetics of ethnicity and nationality, history "now attached to the visibility of the child's body."[16]

During an era featuring great waves of immigration and a somewhat xenophobic desire for social "disease identification and remedy,"[17] the many projects and pedagogical handbooks of the Child-study movement emerged as "the first organized movement to target public school reform in the United States and to deploy the terminology of *centering in* or *on* the child."[18] Children were of particular interest to Child-study behavioral psychologists because in the practice of Child-study, it was believed they were studying the development of the human race. In the aggregation of Child-study data on a pupil, "[l]imb length, jaw angle, health, nationality, and moral 'virtues and perversions' could be recorded on the worksheets provided" and pedagogical inferences could thus be made about what "more could be done to help her or him develop."[19] This data, faulty or not, was important in its communication of the preeminence of modern and classical Western civilization, a powerful worldview that has historically asserted "the absolute superiority of the human over the nonhuman, the masculine over the feminine, the adult over the child, the historical over the ahistorical, and the modern or progressive over the traditional or the savage."[20]

Schools were thus experiments in molding youngsters for the requirements of basic citizenship and to fit the needs of an industrial work force; any resulting vocational assignments were based upon an array of assumptions, ranging from bodily social or ethnic markers to the results of tests of cognitive ability—all interpreted through the delimiting eyes of a student's teachers and administrators. Schools functioned as social factories intended to manage and control their students' behavior, preventing deviance and criminality and rendering students compliant as they became laborers or entered other predetermined employment outcomes. This function of schools has not fundamentally changed to this day, even though children are entering a very different world requiring more creative skills and the MFA is being called the new MBA.[21] This however is clear—public education was never intended to value and develop the creativity potential of learners. What has not been as obvious is the evidence that our prevailing system of public education also appears to actively diminish creative problem solving and community building.

The primary effect of the devaluation of creativity has been the development of citizens limited by a "workbook mentality," individuals cognitively prepared only:

1. to address the set of problems and suggested solutions placed before them by a boss or manager and unable to conceive of self-initiating their own list of things to do or attempt;

2. to do as instructed, unwilling to freelance, troubleshoot, or float outside the lines in search of alternative perspectives;

3. to accept as valid and viable what has been completed in prior exercises, unable to envision the validity or viability of what is not yet visible to anyone else.

A "workbook mentality" emerges from an impoverished, mal-nourished model of education and is a sign of underdeveloped creativity.

I concluded the conversation with my wife's cousin by suggesting that within a model of education that fails to invest in the fullest potential of its students, a completed workbook is not intended as evidence of creativity, but rather as evidence that a set of freight cars filled with pre-sorted understandings has arrived on schedule—just before being dispatched to the next assigned grade level destination. A workbook is an assigned checklist of exercises—students are required to demonstrate the acquisition of predetermined facts and skills, nothing more. A "workbook mentality" pervades a schooling model where the testing and evaluation of learners is not intended to see what each learner has discovered on their own, or has the ability to discover, but rather to see what their teachers have delivered into their heads by that point in time.

In other words, the primary purpose of a completed work-book is to help school managers monitor whether or not the systematic, controlled manipulation of a particular batch (or classroom) of learners has matched a general proposition about what they should know and be able to do after its completion. But rote learning is *boring* and also leads to disengaged learn-ers who are painfully aware that they are not truly being chal-lenged. The consequences are not surprising. Bored learners seek diversions—escapes. At least, when we daydream, we are truly thinking on our own.

Near the beginning of Steven Spielberg's *Jurassic Park*, a character named Dr. Ian Malcolm, an expert in chaos theory, unexpectedly issues the following warning to the scientists attempting to contain and control the genetic codes of the dinosaurs they are cloning and repopulating: "Life will not be contained! Life breaks free, it expands to new territories, and crashes through barriers, painfully, maybe even dangerously, but, ah, well, there it is." In other words, life is fully equipped to behave unpredictably. Like a swarm of salmon swimming upstream, the unpredictable trajectory of individual salmon as they climb ensures that some will be successful in their journey and that those successes will extend the life of their gene pool. Dr. Malcolm was warning that the life cycles of growing herds of dinosaurs, even though bred and hatched only for display on the remote island theme park, could not in the end be controlled from a central bank of computers. Each herd was creating its own ecosystem of behavior and development.

Likewise, individual human destinies cannot be mapped out beforehand because life is subject to the influence of the unexpected successes of the diverse lives to which one is vitally connected. This unpredictability happens to be a hallmark of our collective creativity and it is wonderful to behold in action. Creativity is, after all, the ultimate ripple effect.

IN SUMMARY, SCHOOLS DO WHAT THEY are intended to do—schools underdevelop creativity in favor of the development of citizens who are easy to categorize, easy to sort into cubicles or assembly lines, and easy to manage. Twentieth-century behavioral psychology and the principles of "scientific management" converged in the classrooms across the nation to shape a system of education that penalizes unpredictability and a lack of adherence to prescribed metrics. However, creativity will not be contained. Creativity breaks free, it expands to new territories, and crashes through barriers, painfully, maybe even dangerously. Can we locate creativity's social origin and, if so, how can we better understand its purposes toward the development of learning without containments?

CHAPTER TWO

SOCIAL NETWORKS

A SWARM THEORY
OF CREATIVITY

In hindsight, the immense popularity of Facebook, Google, and YouTube should have been easily predicted. Yes, they are exemplars of what has been termed the World Wide Web 2.0, representing an evolution in social networking beyond passive viewing, featuring user-generated content, participatory information sharing, collaboration, and the building up of virtual communities with a kind of "collective consciousness." However, these modern forms of social media also happen to be the external manifestations of certain behavioral habits common to all successful social creatures—habits of interaction that require no technology at all but which have been further facilitated, accelerated, and amplified through the means of technology in the digital era.

These native social habits are always creative because that is their basic biological function, perpetuating the viability of any living species. For example, like the World Wide Web 2.0, a honeybee swarm *also* features user-generated content (e.g., the honey), participatory information sharing (e.g., the waggle dance communicating to hive-mates which direction to fly for food), collaboration (e.g., the building of a honeycomb for storing honey and eggs), and the building of the colony's specialized bee-to-bee communal relationships.

As indicated in earlier chapters, these behaviors are always on display in human networks and they are also a source of origin in the fostering of human creativity. The main point here is that social networks, small and large, have long pre-existed Facebook and the technology that makes Facebook possible. In fact, social networks are a crucial arena of interaction that continues to aid personal creative growth and the transformation of our social contexts. This chapter's examination of how social networks behave also offers a first glimpse at swarm intelligence in action.

A GATHERING SWARM

In a once-in-a-lifetime turn of events, the networks of Facebook, Google, and YouTube converged on June 10, 2010, as the catalyst of a creative and self-organizing social protest that would change the shape of the nation of Egypt. The impact of this technological convergence communicates a story of unbridled group interaction that is hindered only by the fear of change. The impulse to preserve the stability of the known world will often squelch the emergence of the revolutionary unknowns that creativity tends to unleash.

How does a swarm begin? The advance of a swarm begins just as any creative movement does, with the general disorder and unfocused chaos of life. Scientific observations of the behavior of insects tossed together before coalescing into a swarm show that what is manifested within the disorder is a palpable lack of progress for any of the individual insects, highlighted by collisions with obstacles and other aimless individuals. Biologists have learned that the key to turning the aimlessness of such insects into swarming activity is the enticement of enough individuals to align themselves and move in the same direction. Even if one is not exactly sure where one is going, it beats going nowhere.

Four days prior to June 10, 2010, police in Alexandria savagely beat a young Egyptian businessman named Khaled Said to death in a doorway across the street from the cybercafé where they arrested him. Reports differ as to exactly why Said was murdered (the officers were convicted and received seven-year sentences), but what is agreed is that the beating was emblematic of an Egypt that was going nowhere...stuck in a morass of political and social corruption with no progress in sight. Modern Egypt has a youthful population—about two-thirds of which are 30 years old or under—many of whom are educated, unemployed, and angry about the lack of presidential term limits, the need for increased job opportunities, a higher minimum wage, government reform, and an end to police brutality. Barring the way to progress was a man whom the populace for the most part perceived as a tyrant, a former military commander and sitting autocrat named Hosni Mubarak.

And it came to pass that on June 10, 2010, a convergence of social media platforms was initiated for the common good. A regional Google marketing executive named Wael Ghonim started a Facebook page titled "We are all Khaled Said" carrying YouTube videos with images of a happy Khaled, smiling and alive, contrasted with graphic photos of his smashed face that were smuggled from the morgue. This Facebook page quickly ballooned in membership to become the largest dissident website in Egypt, featuring videos of acts of police brutality and public demonstrations, while serving as an initial mobilizing tool enticing even more Egyptians to pour into the streets demanding a change for the nation.

During the unexpected social upheaval witnessed in the 18-Day Revolution of 2011 and the ensuing overthrow of President Hosni Mubarak, the young Egyptians demanding economic reforms and greater civil liberties could neither be shielded from a world of possibilities nor crushed under a jackboot behind the regime's swiftly lowered iron curtain of news blackouts. This was because the "Arab Spring," the series of revolutionary political upheavals across the Arab world from late 2010 throughout 2011, had been preceded by a digital revolution that had created a thriving social network. Through social media and other networked communications, encouraging stories of successful civil disobedience spreading from Tunisia to Jordan, Oman, and Yemen became immediately available. The confidence was just as contagious—if President Zine El Abidine Ben Ali of Tunisia could be forced to resign, why not President Hosni Mubarak, who had ruled Egypt uncontested for almost 30 years?

Moreover, when as many as 20,000 protestors first started pouring out into the streets of downtown Cairo on January 25, 2011 to demand the resignation of President Mubarak, these tech-savvy digital natives were able to remain remarkably coordinated over the next eighteen days of bloody uprisings and skirmishes against riot police by using Twitter and text messages and satellite television broadcasts to organize and coordinate. Even though

Wael Ghonim would ultimately be arrested and released, internet service blocked, and cell phone coverage dropped across the nation during the crisis, Mubarak's regime was finally toppled. In every flash of swarm intelligence, as occurred during the Arab Spring, what one can do, another can learn to do. No one individual or social grouping presides over the rest—each behaves together for the common good. The intelligence of the moment is both collective and emergent, generating the buzz and potential of a newly discovered insect swarm.

A SWARM THEORY OF THE SOCIAL ORIGINS OF CREATIVITY

Not all swarm behavior is an exercise in swarm intelligence. For example, swarm behavior may be on view in the interaction between a rush of sperm cells and the egg they are fertilizing, but no individual sperm cell is making any conscious decisions or ruling out alternative possibilities; nor will any individual sperm cell ever make a choice that will entice the cluster to intentionally alter their behavior as a whole. It's only when a swarm engages in a cascade of *decision making* that the activity becomes a lesson in collective, social intelligence.

As is the case within the online social networks enabled by Facebook, Google, and YouTube, intelligent decisions are not solely the domain of the individual member, but also of the entire organism. Intelligence is, simply put, the ability to learn. *Any* self-aware and responsive organism, small or large, has the ability to learn—whether that organism is a teamed unit of two or three persons, or a vast social collective constituted of a thousand individual agents or actors. Yes, an individual can learn on his or her own. But collaborative social networks have creative consequences as their compounding social connections work to proliferate opportunities for individual and collective learning.

Just like individuals, family units also learn. Classrooms learn. Businesses learn. As neighborhoods learn, distinct regionalisms and local fads emerge. As nations learn, distinct cultural trends and political systems take hold. Each of these groups learns as a direct consequence of its own swarm of social relations and interactions. Socioculturally speaking, sometimes what a group learns is a benefit not only to itself but also to those in proximity for generations to come. On the other hand, sometimes what a group learns benefits *only* itself and is at the direct expense of its neighbors.

Educational psychologist Richard S. Prawat has described a problem that has vexed educators and learning theorists for years, a problem that has been termed as the "learning paradox."[1] The paradox itself has been discussed as far back as the days of Plato and Socrates. How are learners "able to leap ahead of what is known in the search for new understanding" given that new understanding "depends on prior learning" and that when new knowledge "is incompatible with this learning, one lacks a base on which to build?"[2] And yet it happens all the time. Even a child can do it. Those attempting to describe this paradox must ultimately address how it is that a new and more sophisticated knowledge base might be fashioned out of prior, less complex knowledge. One way to expand the capacity of one's knowledge base is cumulative. In the popular television show and movie series *Star Trek*, an amoral civilization known as the Borg is a recurring and powerful enemy of the peaceful Federation of Planets. As a society of cyborgs, the Borg are an amalgamation of genetically unrelated humanoid species distinguished by having been networked together through nanotechnology into a single collective consciousness modeled upon the idea of a swarm. The more planets the Borg invade and the more humanoids the Borg civilization forcibly assimilates, the more formidable its cybernetic knowledge base grows to be, and the greater the capacity for the entire Borg collective to acquire and assimilate even more knowledge.

But there are far more moral ways to achieve the growth of collective intelligence. There is an expanding surface area to any organism's intelligence, like the creases of a growing brain, or the undulations of a growing horde of fire ants on the move. As surface area expands, so also does the ability to accumulate and assimilate new intelligence and new potential connectivity. While typically more benign than a marching swarm of fire ants—or the Borg collective—a game of baseball, double Dutch, or soccer nevertheless assembles a swarm of concentrated social activity and collective consciousness. The accumulation of the various abilities and intelligences of each youngster adds to the possibilities of each game.

The dynamics of a swarm's cumulative intelligence and collective behavior are mirrored en masse by the communal ability of Facebook's massive membership to draw new faces into proximity because of a shared desire to engage in a dialogue, play a game, or participate in an event. Similarly, Google's search engine spiders' crawl across the web browsing the number of relevant associated pages that link to any given site that is returned in a search result. Twitter casts free-associative nets marrying a hot topic, a voice on that topic, *and* a tuned-in audience. YouTube's facilitation of user-generated video content is shared like the sand in a playground sandbox. These examples are not meant to discount individual agency in the stock of human creativity. But the reality is that social networks operate as *creative contagions*—as natural biosystemic forces communicating individual development through social contact and often the most subtle interactions, whether in the classroom or in the cultural world. As such, our social networks do more to cultivate individual talent/genius than we realize. Ultimately, purpose-driven individual creativity is incubated within systems of social interaction involving a swarm of thinkers and doers.

THE STORY OF THE MOTOWN PHENOMENA presents a useful example here. A record label launched by Detroit entrepreneur Berry Gordy, Jr. in 1960, Motown's founders envisioned it as an assembly line for musical hits. The name Motown itself was a portmanteau of the city's "Motor Town" nickname as well as a reference to the city's reputation as the hub of automobile production for the nation. Yes, Motown created stars and hit singing groups who dominated the pop charts, but those stars and hit groups each reproduced what came to be known as the "Motown Sound" that was largely synonymous with the hugely influential R&B urban dance music genre.[3]

The melodies of Motown were memorable, built to sound best on car stereos or transistor radios.[4] In fact, the Motown Sound was first assembled in a musical hit factory that came to be known as "The Snakepit" located down the street from an immense Cadillac assembly plant. This little row house on Detroit's West Grand Boulevard served as the main headquarters of Motown, including its rehearsal space as well as recording studios. Most importantly, the manufacturing of this collective sound—despite the well-marketed prominence of Berry Gordy's name—was a brilliantly successful collaboration between a small network of Black businessmen and women including *numerous* musicians, songwriters, performers, producers, and recording engineers, many of whose names remain obscure even today. Within their "Snakepit" lair, this small and tightly knit social network eventually grew to occupy a group of houses anointed as "Hitsville U.S.A." New recording artists, new hit songs, and newly packaged vinyl records were all produced quickly in an assembly-line procession, with contributions from each member of the Motown collective. And they were made rigorously well, so that consumers would keep coming back for more.

> Somewhat infamously, Berry Gordy subjected his artists to rigorous training—not just as singers, but as young men and young ladies, and as entertainers. They learned to comport themselves with well-bred dignity. They learned how to walk, how to speak, and how to use a salad fork. They learned not just to hit the right notes, but to handle a microphone, to move with grace onstage, to project an air of respectability. Gordy, you see, envisioned his stable of artists playing not on the storied "chitlin circuit" but in theaters and stadiums, not just on the radio but on television and in the movies. Ultimately, they did.[5]

In any social network, mentorship matters. It is easy to remember the many individual artists—like the precocious boy musician Stevie Wonder, or Diana Ross, once the lead singer of the Supremes until she went solo—who emerged from the prolific Motown social network of activity. But Motown also serves as a clear model of how individual artistry emerges from collective creative interaction and strong mentorship; participation in collective acts of creativity leaves an imprint of residual traits upon the individual. Creativity draws upon the widest possible spectrum of experiences, behaviors, and attributes. This breadth would not be possible if creativity did not also arise from the collective arena of experiences and points of view not initially our own, yet permanently imprinting us with contagious new traits. Collective creativity is in turn accelerated by the momentum of individual creators who find their highest purposes achieved as their achievements redirect the attentions and cultural trajectory of the larger social group. The catalyst for that redirection can be as subtle as an individual's interaction with a timely invention, a provocative piece of writing, or a well-timed hit song.

WHETHER IN GENERAL SOCIETY, BUSINESS CIRCLES, or classrooms, the relationship between the swarm intelligence of the social network and the multiple intelligences of its individual creators is always symbiotic. This relationship is a collective and generative behavior that simultaneously fosters the development of individual thinkers and the larger cultures they constitute.

Swarm intelligence shapes the growth of insect hordes, animal herds, schools of fish, and human communities alike. It is a higher order of thinking than automatic impulses or unconscious instinct and affects the behavior of the many as well as the one. In some contexts, we call swarm intelligence "mob mentality." Sometimes we call it "peer pressure." Sometimes we call swarm intelligence "group dynamics" or "herd behavior" or "crowd hysteria." Swarm intelligence is on display in every classroom and school you enter, on every pedestrian walkway and congested highway. It is fundamental to every advertising campaign, every focus group, and every business-to-business or business-to-consumer operation. Sometimes it's not very intelligent at all—it can be the bleating of sheep being led to their slaughter. Or it can be the herd of lemmings charging blindly over the cliffside.

Like any intelligence, swarm intelligence involves conscious choices toward the yield of newly learned understandings and behaviors. In the most positive contexts, those choices are distributed across multiple agents serving to the advantage of those individuals while no less serving to the mutual benefit of the whole cohort if and when others choose to move in a similar direction, receive the same stimuli, acquire the same information, or adopt similar behaviors. In the worst circumstances, swarm intelligence is stunted and curtailed, reduced to only the most regimented behavior through means of both benign interference and invasive reconditioning. The more closed, parochial, or conservative a society becomes and the less willing it is to open borders and invite new connections, the lesser its capability of fostering inventiveness and creativity. Ideological stances that promote individualism or present barriers to new gene pools of thought also stifle the free movement of creative waves across the social landscape. In other words, hyper-conservatism, homogeneity, and zenophobia all have larger creative consequences.

A swarm commences when individuals are enticed to align in undertaking a significant change in trajectory or behavior that is more beneficial or gratifying than the prior trajectory or behavior. The expanded intelligence of any swarm as it collectively learns and replicates an expedient action or behavior is typically manifested as an altered state of action or consciousness. This altered state may become immediately apparent to the observer—as when observing the shape-shifting patterns of a large soaring flock of starlings, or the quicksilver darts of a streaking school of tuna, or the undulating surface of a teeming colony of ants on the move;

conversely, an altered state of being may best present itself only after the duration of time—as when taking measure of the piling up of waters at high tide, the flow of an artic glacier, or the etching of a canyon by a vast, unceasing river.

How does the behavior of a swarm appear to the beholder? As the primary point of origin of collective and individual creativity, it is vital to be able to identify swarm intelligence when it is happening right in front of our eyes—and just as importantly, when it is being disrupted. To the most careful observer, swarm intelligence manifests itself in all cases upon our planet as a sustained, successive pattern of purposeful physical or metaphysical movement. As in a vast rolling herd or a migration of birds, the swarm intelligence of a human social network motivates proximate bodies in apparent coordination, even as it activates partnering minds in concert. The awareness of patterns like these is crucial; like the Periodic Table of chemical elements, social patterns reveal underlying structure and help us to figure out origins and categories of being and why we behave as we do.

The activation of a swarm is sustained as long as it solves the need for new direction, growth, development, or mutual gratification. Once forward momentum, growth, development or mutual gratification is halted even in spite of the swarm's continued behavior, the individual actors within the swarm are once again compelled toward the chaos of myriad self-determined actions in search of a satisfactory outcome. Any discernible pattern of behavior will continue to disintegrate until enough individual actors are enticed to align in accord with some newly advantageous discovery. These principles will be elaborated in later chapters.

Given the scope of these principles, any social emphasis on the achievement of greater swarm intelligence and cultural cohesion is a cycle that ideally repeats itself. Yet unless the natural erosion of cohesive behavior is rebooted to become a whole new swarm of creative activity, collective intelligence easily deteriorates and mutually beneficial cultural developments begin to come to a halt. Individuals begin to deprioritize the benefits of behaving together creatively, instead placing an emphasis on the individual pursuit of happiness and the erroneous assumption of sole responsibility for personal achievements. A unified social emphasis on the common good weakens considerably.

The collective energy of human creative output, expressed as human cultural achievements, ebbs and surges like recurrent weather patterns. If you can discern a pattern, you can discern the underlying structure that will replicate it. The gathering of a swarm is like the development of a turbulent cloud formation with the potential to unleash a thousand individual lightning bolts to illuminate the sky. Just as impressively, in society as in nature, our collected human social energy also produces the most powerful individual flashes. We may call them prodigies or geniuses, or treat them like once-in-a-lifetime streaks of light across the nighttime sky, but they always emerge from the leading edge of a swarm of thinkers who think very much like they do. What is the underlying structure that produces creative thinking?

PRINCIPLES OF SWARM INTELLIGENCE AT WORK IN AN ART LESSON

In his book *The Smart Swarm*, author Peter Miller outlines some fascinating principles about the collective, self-organizing, and adaptive behavior of swarms that will also aid our understanding of the social origins of human creativity. Creative behavior exceeds self-expression; it is more than being "the expression of an individual," more than "personal creativity." It is the development of the social hive that shelters and supports the success of the local collective and the lone individual alike. As a senior editor of *National Geographic*—and possessing an acute awareness of how much we have yet to understand about one of the most common and natural social behaviors—Miller draws upon observations of intelligent swarms of ants, termites, honeybees, and other social creatures *behaving together* within their natural habitats.

Using another analogy, when we test for individual intelligence in schools, we are actually looking at a Richter scale graph charting creative social earthquakes and their ensuing aftershocks. We usually look at the needle dancing across the page as if that is what matters most, but it's not. What matters most are the tectonic shifts between human beings as they interact and cause the needle to jump. In other words, standardized test scores that record a jump in the needle are not primarily the evidence of that individual's achievement, but of the reverberating achievements of a student's peer groups, family, classrooms, and surrounding society—causing aftershocks of creative intelligence that linger productively in the individual psyche. Even subtle interactions between a teacher and the student may cause the needle to respond vigorously. In the aftershock of cultural achievement, the *social* landscape is left changed and individuals are mobilized in response.

I have long held the conviction that I learned everything I needed to know about teaching creativity and the arts in education from the first complete art lesson I ever taught as I completed my graduate studies at Teachers College, Columbia University. I completed my student teaching practicum experience at Hunter

College Elementary School where I also worked as director of that school's extended-day enrichment program. Under the supervision of master art teacher Anne Rosenthal, I taught an elementary school art class for the first time to a group of first graders, but the lessons I learned are just as enduring as they were fundamental. I believe there are larger implications about human creative behavior hidden within the layers of a teaching and learning experience lived long ago. Sketching out some of Peter Miller's observations about smart swarms on top of some personal reflections about the art-making activity of my first grade students, I think I can accurately portray the workings of a creative swarm.

The art lesson was a sculpture project designed for a first grade class with approximately twelve children at a time taking part in the activity. The lesson's aim, or learning objective, was for students to figure out how to create a sculpture of a person or animal that could stand on its own using only found wood scraps. Our previous activity was a paper collage project and so the students were familiar with the idea of scavenging for assorted pieces of material and assembling them into something meaningful. Effective learning opportunities build upon prior learning. I placed crates of wood scraps on the floor next to each large worktable, along with bottles of wood glue, rolls of masking tape, watercolor trays, paintbrushes and buttons so they were accessible.

I began by showing students a picture of a particular sculpture from a book of black and white photos titled *The Sculpture of Picasso*. As a motivating topic question intended to "hook" the interest of each student I asked, "Why does Picasso use forks to make hands instead of just cutting his hands out of wood?"

Responses included the important observation that the forks *already* looked like fingers. As an association question intended to guide each student toward deeper mental connections with the significant idea at the center of the lesson, I then held up a piece of scrap wood and asked: "What part of a person or animal could this piece of wood be if you used your imagination?" I had anticipated that responses might range from a shoulder, to a cow's head, to an ear, to a foot, to a nose, to an elbow. I allowed the excited student responses to propel the discussion and generate further dialogue.

I then asked a visualization question intended to direct student thinking toward showing, depicting, or representing any divergent ideas that had emerged in mind during the prior segment of the lesson discussion. One or two adventurous students were asked to come pick an oddly shaped piece of wood and suggest what it might be. I asked the rest of the class to anticipate what shapes might be lurking in the other crates around the room, and gave each student advance permission to search a crate near another table only if they could not find the right shape needed in the crate nearest to them.

Finally, I asked several transition questions preceded by simple directives aimed at moving learners in an orderly fashion from visualizing what they might do to actually doing it. Students were challenged to remember:

1. to make a sculpture of a person or animal;
2. to choose three pieces of wood to start with from the nearest crate and make them stand;
3. to remember that the rule for gluing two pieces of wood together is "flat against flat."

Before dismissing students from the discussion circle, I asked: "What pieces of wood will *you* choose? How will you put them together to make them stand? What piece will you put at the bottom? What pieces can you use as feet?" And for good measure, I reminded them that they could always go back for more wood or even exchange pieces with someone else. I then sent students to their assigned tables and the quietest students at the quietest tables were given permission two at a time to pluck choice wood scraps from nearby crates. At appropriate points during the work period, I demonstrated the gluing process to the kids and showed them how they could use the masking tape to temporarily bind two pieces of wood together while the glue was drying. Each sculpture project was assembled and painted over the course of at least two class sessions. Upon reflection, every principle of swarm behavior was on display during this learning activity: self-organization, a diversity of knowledge, indirect collaboration, and adaptive mimicking.

A SELF-ORGANIZING QUALITY

A major principle of swarm behavior is *self-organization* within a social network. The evidence of this self-organization is visible in three distinct social behaviors, none of which can be imposed by a queen bee, a leading ant, a master teacher, or a business CEO. In a self-organizing social network, the common "patterns, shapes, and behaviors we see…don't come from preexisting blueprints or designs, but emerge on their own, from the bottom up, as a result of interactions among their many parts."[6] The mechanisms of self-organization are very simple and they are three-fold: *decentralized control, distributed problem-solving,* and *multiple interactions between agents*. Self-organization is said to be the source both of evolutionary variety and system resilience, the ability to survive any unexpected changes in the environment.

Decentralized control is a self-organizing characteristic of swarm intelligence wherein its individual members act with autonomy, behaving together without orchestration, "free to make their own decisions within a relatively sparse set of restrictions" imposed by their teachers or business leaders.[7] In the first grade learning activity, control over student project outcomes was decentralized. Decentralization is at its most visible within the midst of a social network of activity and is self-organizing; it looks messy and at times chaotic. The sculpture lesson was constructed to cede to the students any jurisdiction I might have exerted over their creative decisions due to my position as the authority figure in the room. Instead, students were free to make any person or animal their materials allowed them to imagine as long as it was able to stand on its own.

Distributed problem solving is a self-organizing characteristic of swarms wherein each individual group member "contributes a bit towards creating a solution" rather than relying on a parent, manager, or other authority figure to entirely work out the problem for them.[8] It is crucial to understand that this problem-solving behavior does not need to be altogether simultaneous, with all individuals working together on a single project outcome toward one collective "aha!" moment; rather, this quality of swarm intelligence may just as readily be distributed over time, with each individual ultimately contributing a separate outcome toward a deepened overall understanding of the wide range of possible project outcomes, ultimately extending the vision of every group member. In this first grade sculpture activity, each student was free to solve the problem differently. There was no one correct solution any individual student might conceive—no one right animal or person or pose or color choice. In fact, individual achievement was not the goal, even though individual achievements were certainly accomplished along the way. The primary goal was to build the group's creative social intelligence—while overcoming gravity's propensity for toppling objects little kids put their hands on in the real world.

The self-organizing characteristic of swarms also requires *multiple interactions* wherein autonomous individuals take full advantage of opportunities to "interact frequently and in a variety of different ways."[9] Earlier, I introduced the notion of how cultures are slowly created as individual members of social groups deploy the biocultural markers of their most rewarding choices and successful solutions for others to model after. The markers and models of social benefit may be products of artistry, design, science, or human service. All are equally of value toward the development of an enduring culture. These social markers work like the excreted or secreted chemical attractors in ant colonies, working to entice other individuals to adopt learned habits, behavioral patterns, and useful inventions. Peter Miller points out that these markers—and the successes they point to—can be easy to overlook in the hustle and bustle of everyday activity...whether inside of an anthill, a classroom, or a business office. Multiple interactions between group members help to "amplify faint but important signals and speed up decision making."[10] In my first grade art class, students were encouraged to have multiple interactions with classmates by periodically leaving their seats and floating around the classroom looking at each other's work, asking questions, and even helping each other with their gluing as needed. In this way, a mini-culture of first-time sculptors was mutually achieved.

THE MYTH OF THE LONE GENIUS

A second major principle of swarm behavior is *a diversity of knowledge* within a social network. The meaning of diversity is variety, not disunity, since unified purpose is indeed possible amongst a heterogeneous social network of autonomous thinkers and doers. Peter Miller draws upon the research of economist Scott Page in discussing the incredible power of cognitive diversity to sense a new avenue of possibility when most everyone is stuck with the same solutions.

> When a group is struggling with a difficult problem, it helps if each member brings a mix of tools to the job. That's why, increasingly, scientists collaborate on interdisciplinary teams, and why companies seek out bright employees who haven't all graduated from the same schools....But when people with diverse problem-solving skills put their heads together, they often outperform groups of the smartest individuals. Diversity, in short, trumps ability.[11]

Close, but not quite. More accurately, diversity *enhances* ability. Diversity is capable of drawing out long-dormant ideas and latent talents into newfound utility as each is brought into proximity with someone now able to make use of what once seemed to contradict all common sense. The well-known axiom of the "great idea before its time" is a terrible misnomer; all good ideas are a product of their times. Those who fail to advance good ideas— whether those ideas are discovered or constructed one element at a time—are like the lone scout insect that is unable or unwilling to return to the hive or colony and share all that it has learned.

The greatest known example is the tragedy of the classic "Renaissance Man" Leonardo da Vinci. Before his death in 1519, Leonardo produced a portfolio of hundreds of brilliantly realized anatomical drawings of dissected corpses, dogs, frogs, horses, bears, monkeys, and bats, completed from around 1490 to the early 1500s. Leonardo's incisive studies of the workings of the human heart from the years 1511 to 1513 are said to astound cardiac surgeons even to this day. Leonardo's artistic pen-and-ink renderings were so carefully observed and full of discoveries that they would have changed the history of science and medicine had they been published during his lifetime. Instead, they were bequeathed to an assistant and disappeared from view for hundreds of years. Leonardo's penchant for secretiveness did not stop there. He was a known procrastinator and if his paintings weren't perfect in his own estimation, he often destroyed them. As a practicing architect, musician, anatomist, inventor, engineer, sculptor, mathematician, and painter, when Leonardo sketched out his creations in his notebooks he often left out essential steps just to confuse anyone who might be interested in following in his footsteps. He also wrote in a shorthand code called "mirror writing," inking his sentences backward and his letters from left to right, while also breaking up his words and phrases in arbitrary places.

It is safe to presume that Leonardo's first and foremost motivation was *not* to share his ideas and inventions freely with his neighbors and fellow Renaissance thinkers. At least, not until he was good and ready. And for all his genius, that's perhaps the one problem that he failed to solve. There is never an optimal time to share with the rest of the hive; most won't even pay attention at the time you choose to do so. But the fact that diversity is a messy and oftentimes thankless social arrangement should not be misconstrued as a signal that some in the group are at a deficit in comparison to others and unworthy of networking; in fact, the purpose of diversity is to expand the gene pool of available ideas and abilities in a cross-fertilizing exchange…sometimes with alarming suddenness and sometimes very gradually, as if by osmosis. It is a response to the reality that no individual can be and do all things.

Creativity does not happen in a vacuum. The "lone genius" is a myth; Leonardo did not come out of nowhere and he did not learn on his own. Apprenticed at the age of fourteen to the artist Andrea del Verrocchio, who worked for the court of the powerful Florentine statesman and arts patron Lorenzo de' Medici, Leonardo was the product of a swarm of activity that was known as one of the finest workshops in all of Florence, Italy, producing several other artists who grew to fame. According to a Wikipedia entry, Leonardo's young mind was "exposed to both theoretical training and a vast range of technical skills including drafting, chemistry, metallurgy, metal working, plaster casting, leather working, mechanics and carpentry as well as the artistic skills of drawing, painting, sculpting and modeling" at Verrocchio's very well-funded workshop.[12] By the age of twenty, Leonardo was qualified as a master in the Guild of Saint Luke, a guild of artists and doctors of medicine highlighting an era when there was no false division or hierarchy between the intellectual value or practice of the arts and sciences.

Individuals must interact with other minds, even if that interaction takes place as the page of a book is activated in the mind of a reader. Sadly, Leonardo did not publish his findings in anatomy, civil engineering, optics, or hydrodynamics although he himself was an avid reader. Minds like Leonardo's ignite easily and burn long and brightly. Likewise, Leonardo could have been an extraordinary catalyst for the advancement of thinking in the scientific circles of his contemporaries. Alas, while famous as an artist at the time, Leonardo was no direct influence at all upon the scientific thinking in his day and age.

Frankly, we need each other. Any individual stands to gain from the next. We need the differences between us to alter our life experiences and possibilities by association, reshaping the culture that provides our context for understanding the world—or just reframing the task directly in front of us. We need proximity and access to one another's biases and interests in order to help us see the possibilities beyond our *own* biases and interests. New knowledge is the outcome of each new interpretation of individual or social life experience that proximity brings. For all that Leonardo da Vinci means to the world today because of his individual achievements, he would have meant a whole lot more to his world centuries ago if he had regularly sought to help diversify the knowledge of *all* his contemporaries, not just his artistic apprentices—even if his ideas were less than perfect and his many inventions could not yet be tested.

The evidence of a diversity of knowledge at work within a swarm is visible in four distinct social characteristics and manifestations that are each dependent upon the diversity of group members, life experiences, and/or work functions. First, the diversity of knowledge within swarms requires heterogeneity, the bringing together of "individuals with a wide range of backgrounds and cognitive abilities."[13] The more random the congregation of individuals, the better. This is why cities, like corporations, have so often been at the center of great social and technological innovations and breakthroughs. In the case of my first grade art class, the life experiences and interests of my diverse students were varied. The discussion at the start of the lesson was intended to trigger enough divergent responses to avoid any possibility of students attempting to satisfy any one individual's conception of a single correct solution—even the teacher's!

Second, the diversity of knowledge within swarms also provides a means of escape from the limits of human intuition. Human intuition and gut instinct are wonderful as far as they go, but even if you are Leonardo da Vinci, intuition needs to be reignited and supplemented. Reignited curiosity and supplemented thinking both require outside catalysts and resources, especially in the face of complex problems. The key to igniting the learning activity I presented to my first graders was the initial dialogue and guiding questions, which was intended to dislodge possibilities for animals and persons that might be assembled right along with the scrap wood. The key to reigniting the activity when students started to lose their focus was to stop and talk about the small sculptures being erected from tabletop to tabletop.

In the same way that "society counts on groups to be more reliable than individuals," the intelligence of the swarm is intended to be greater than the intelligence of individual group members. The common sense of juries, committees, corporate boards, and governmental advisory panels is expected to supersede all the good sense any one individual can muster; likewise the collective creativity of a classroom, a design think tank, or a cultural collective far exceeds the creativity of a single woman, man or child and never fails to inspire.

Third, the diversity of knowledge within swarms invariably invites a friendly competition of ideas jockeying for attention. Peter Miller describes how a swarm of honeybees deliberates over the complex decision of hunting for a new home and relocating the entire population. In order for there to be effective group problem solving, there must be a diversity of individuals with each member of the group providing unique information to the rest of the swarm. The more members of the community persuaded by the potential of one individual's solution to the need at hand, the more time and energy is invested into trying out that particular solution, and the more likely it is to become the answer for all involved. Thus, as ideas *compete* for space in the community's psyche, it becomes a learning community. Miller writes:

> The more choices, the better. By sending out hundreds of scouts at a time, each swarm collected a wealth of information about the neighborhood and the nest boxes, and it did so in a distributed and decentralized way. None of the bees tried to visit [all of the possibilities for a new home] to rate which one was the best. Nor did they submit their findings to some executive committee for a final decision, as workers in a corporation might do. Instead, these hundreds of scouts each provided unique information about the various sites to the group as a whole...[14]

Every scout served as an agent for the advancement of the whole swarm and after evaluating the potential nest site for herself, each bee returned to the hive to broadcast her findings with a brief but vigorous figure-eight "waggle dance" in which the number of circuits performed was intended to communicate the exact distance and trajectory of the possible relocation site. The strength and length of the dances that were the most protracted and exaggerated, some lasting for up to five minutes, were an advertisement of success aimed at enticing as many others as possible toward a similar excitement over an individual scout's information. The number of other hive members willing to follow through on their buzzing enthusiasm and immediately support the viability of a possible relocation site by making the excursion themselves served as the best evidence of how successful each scout had been at the fine art of persuasion. During my sculpture lesson, activity was purposely halted at varying stages not only to look at the emerging ideas, but to get excited by them and draw upon them.

Finally, the diversity of knowledge within swarms is aided by effective mechanisms for narrowing choices. In my classroom, the limits to the art activity that helped to narrow choices for my students included the instruction that each first grader had to use the same materials, that each bin had a finite amount of wood scraps, that three of the scraps had to be selected to start the construction of the sculpture—all of this ensured an economy of thought processing. Each student also had a limited workspace (along with the admonition to be very mindful and respectful of the workspace of one's neighbors), ensuring an economy of size of each final project; the limited availability of my mentorship in helping each assembly to hold together as glue was adhering; and a limited amount of time in each classroom session in order to complete the sculpture in its entirety.

In society, paradigms are the primary mechanism for narrowing choices. A paradigm is "a body of beliefs and values, laws, and practices which govern a community."[15] Scientific historian Thomas S. Kuhn surmised that paradigms develop because of their success in representing the prevailing understandings, shared beliefs, and research solutions of a community.[16] The prevailing paradigm on a subject dictates how people have agreed to think about it...but it also limits our ability to conceive of it otherwise and learn something new about it. Fortunately, when "new information cannot be integrated into the existing paradigm or when problems persist which cannot be resolved," a new paradigm is likely to arise to replace it.[17]

For example, it is easy to assume that the paradigm of "science" as we understand it today was the same held by all those who contributed to what we identify as the "Scientific Revolution" in Western Europe. This assumption is incorrect. Rather, from the fourteenth to approximately the mid-nineteenth century, the prevailing concept of inquiry was "something called 'natural philosophy,' which aimed to describe and explain the entire system of the world."[18] This study of the workings of nature and the physical universe was exemplified in the development of areas of inquiry such as chemistry, astronomy, physics, anatomy, botany, zoology, geology, and mineralogy.

Natural philosophy research practices were intended to harness the constituent elements and forces of nature and the universe through their categorization, measurement, and control— capturing them for humanity's benefit. It is easy to forget that this effort to develop methods to control nature's constitutive elements and define the laws governing the natural world was analogous to the methods developed and technical skills applied in Renaissance visual arts, sculpture, and architecture.[19] In other words, as exemplified by artist-researchers like Leonardo Da Vinci, Western art-making served as "an instrument of knowledge."[20] The creative and the scientific were raised together in human culture as siblings.

Early in the Scientific Revolution, when Galileo asked the question, "Did the sun and the stars really revolve around the earth?," he ultimately discovered that our planet is not the center of the universe, and the answer to his question changed the way the whole world thinks today. A paradigm shift is a creative force within a culture. But because a paradigm is an agreed way of thinking, an individual cannot change it alone. It takes a whole swarm to narrow a host of possibilities down to a new paradigm that will govern its behavior for the time being. Moreover, a paradigm shift does not accelerate across a culture and spill over borders without an accompanying signal that awakens the whole social hive, like a change in the human body's sympathetic nervous system priming the body for action in response to a *fight-or-flight* stimulus—the cultural equivalent to elevated blood pressure, goose bumps, or a sudden flow of sweat. When a change is coming, all of society seems to come to attention, like households surrounding their television sets and radios during the unfolding events of the United States Civil Rights Movement.

In summary, behave like you're part of a social network—*become awake to who you are not and what you cannot yet do, and then expand your thinking and actions in sympathetic response to the behavior of those who are unlike yourself.* In the next chapter, some of civilization's most important sociocultural achievements—and failures—will be reviewed as the historical evidence of swarm intelligence and how it adapts our social worlds.

CHAPTER THREE

SYSTEMS

HOW SWARM INTELLIGENCE ADAPTS OUR SOCIAL WORLDS

When societies and nations misbehave, each is capable of destroying not only itself, but its neighbors and natural habitats as well. As I was preparing to write this chapter, I encountered a brief video on Vimeo about the strange thing that happens to astronauts as they view the earth through a spaceship window for the very first time. These astronauts experience what is called "the overview effect" wherein it becomes suddenly obvious that the entire planet, and every human in it, is one vast and unified living system.

Standing on the Earth's surface, we are fettered not only by gravity, but by the boundaries of our senses, our localities, and our inherited philosophies and worldviews. In stark contrast, any view from an orbiting space station window or capsule provides a clarifying overview of our interactive planetary ecosystems—with only the thinnest layer of fragile atmosphere protecting us all from cosmic oblivion. Any personal doubts about how changes in the environment on one part of the planet can affect the climate on another part of the planet suddenly disappear.

Unfortunately, most of us will never gain the perspective of "the overview effect" by becoming astronauts or viewing the Earth from beyond its atmosphere. And yet unless we find a shared big picture perspective that galvanizes a collective awareness that we are all in this together, our ability to behave accordingly often fails to coalesce. Consequently, it is all too easy to destroy much more of our habitat and communal relationships than any collaborative solution can remedy long before we learn to get a handle on our worst misbehaviors.

The misbehavior that is bound to have the most enduring consequences is our failure to consistently behave together to achieve the greater common good. Each individual person, nation, or subculture stubbornly maintains self-interests as an overriding priority. We find it difficult to hold the big picture in mind. Toward that aim, the remainder of this book is written to provide the catalyst for a viral "overview effect," expanding our collective perspective beyond prior limitations. In this chapter, I will present an overview of how swarm intelligence shapes our social worlds.

GENERATIVE SYSTEMS OF HUMAN BEHAVIOR

A third major principle of swarm intelligence is *indirect collaboration* within a social network. In *JAZZ*, an award-winning PBS documentary series, director Ken Burns pokes some additional holes into the Western mythology of the lone, isolated genius.

We still wrestle with this myth as if producing an outstanding composer like Duke Ellington, or a breathtaking cornet player like Louis Armstrong is the ultimate achievement of creativity. Ken Burns makes the counterargument that *collaborative systems* were more of a key to the development of jazz than the effort to stand out from the crowd or to be a lone ranger. In the early days of jazz, "cutting contests" served as a form of competitive engagement on various levels of musicianship—sometimes between aspiring high school students, sometimes between professional musicians, and sometimes between the heavyweight musical artists in a region—wherein each musician would try to top the other in a battle to shift local axes of power and prestige. Keith Sawyer writes the following about his experience as a jazz musician in a brief discussion of his 2008 book, *Group Genius: The Creative Power of Collaboration*:

> My years of playing piano in jazz ensembles convinced me that what happened in any one person's mind could never explain what made one night's performance shine and another a dud. At any second during a performance, an almost invisible musical exchange could take the piece in a new direction; later, no one could remember who was responsible for what. In jazz, the group has the ideas, not the individual musicians.[1]

In a similar vein, Duke Ellington and Louis Armstrong did not appear out of nowhere—they emerged from the complex clash of sociocultural systems that each in its own way contributed to the birth of jazz in New Orleans. Jazz emerged from the most cosmopolitan city of the nineteenth century, where on any given day one could hear the sound of brass marching bands, spirituals of the

Black church, Italian opera, traveling minstrel shows, the offbeat accents and swing rhythms of ragtime, the New Orleans blues, Caribbean-influenced piano salon music, Afro-Cuban habanera music, Creole concert bands, and popular European music hall performances. Ellington and Armstrong emerged from the indirect collaboration between these various swarms of musical activity, which ultimately gave birth to the invention of jazz. Ellington and Armstrong, in turn, would go on to shift the entire trajectory of American popular culture.

The indirect collaboration of New Orleans musical artists and musical forms produced an emergent creative process we now call jazz. Jazz performance has had many iterations and styles, from big band to be-bop to fusion; each has been a demonstration of a unique creative process within a larger system of improvisatory behavior. The purpose of any system of human behavior—whether aesthetic, scientific, political, or economic—is to be fruitful and to perpetuate itself, producing new forms, information, and social transformation. The swarm intelligence at work in the indirect collaboration of the aesthetic, scientific, political, and economic systems that human beings create also realigns our best ideas and practices, changing our social worlds.

Not surprisingly, the contemporary business world has also caught on to the benefits of indirect collaboration. A 2013 issue of *Fast Company* magazine highlights the swarm-based social networking trend of "coworking," a practice where companies plan for their employees to share office spaces with strangers employed by other companies. Coworking has been discovered anew as a means for developing latent talents within workers, yielding new creative collaborations and increasing efficiency in getting products to market—it combines the benefits of cooperation for success and competition for success into one synergistic multi-hive.

According to the *Fast Company* article "Working Beyond the Cube," strategies for coworking tend to fall into three categories: (1) individual-to-individual where diverse employees and self-employed freelancers are invited to cross paths regularly and draw upon each other's resources in shared, multi-purpose, flexible-use watering hole–type office spaces; (2) company-to-company sharing "in which a group of companies pool space, employees, and ideas"; (3) and private-to-public sharing, "inviting outsiders to work inside your company building or campus."[2]

What if we were to survey the changes in human behavior as we work together in a longitudinal study from the window of a space capsule overhead? What would we see? I propose that when individuals from one social network interface with individuals from another social network, the larger changes resulting from this behavior are the consequence of worldviews merging—sending a ripple effect of feedback loops back and forth throughout each system and thereby altering the big picture for all of us.

A STORY OF CREATIVE SOCIAL SYSTEMS IN HUMAN HISTORY

In her remarkable book *Thinking in Systems*, Donella H. Meadows defines a system as a "set of elements or parts that is coherently organized and interconnected in a pattern or structure" that becomes more than the sum of its parts and "produces a characteristic set of behaviors" classified as its "function" or "purpose."[3]

Meadows eloquently describes how many kinds of systems surround us every day and how simply and elegantly they behave:

> A school is a system. So is a city, and a factory, and a corporation, and a national economy....A tree is a system, and a forest is a larger system that encompasses subsystems of trees and animals. The earth is a system...so is a galaxy. Systems can be embedded in systems, which are embedded in yet other systems....When a living creature dies, it loses its "system-ness." The multiple interrelations that held it together no longer function, and it dissipates....Systems can change, adapt, respond to events, seek goals, mend injuries, and attend to their own survival in lifelike ways, although they may contain or consist of nonliving things. Systems can be self-organizing, and often are self-repairing over at least some range of disruptions. They are resilient, and many of them are evolutionary. Out of one system other completely new, never-before-imagined systems can arise.[4]

A system of social behavior has multiple elements or parts that interconnect to serve a particular purpose for a group of people. For example, about 12,000 years ago, most human social groups consisted of hunters and gatherers. This required a nomadic existence over a relatively large territorial range where one part of the group—the hunters—tracked and trailed behind herds of wild game for miles, and the other part of the group—the gatherers—constantly sought new areas from which to gather in preparation for when the food supplies growing from trees and other plant life in a given location were plucked clean and exhausted. The purpose of hunting and gathering was simply to stay alive.

But because all human social activity has a tendency to erode and dissipate in its focus and effectiveness, it is "the consistent behavior pattern over a long period of time that is the first hint of the existence of a feedback loop."[5] In this case, I am referring to the kind of self-regulating condition wherein a system has the ability to stabilize itself within an acceptable pattern range that maintains its survival by feeding back some of its constitutive elements into its own stock in a kind of loop. The stock in any given system "are the elements of the system that you can see, feel, count, or measure at any given time."[6] The stock in a social network of hunter-gatherers is its population. Stocks respond to change somewhat gradually, even sudden change, because the nature of a system is to be resilient and conserve its identity.

The stock in a system also serves as the memory bank of changes to its accumulation to that point in time—sometimes rapidly accumulating or developing, sometimes diminishing toward dissipation or extinction, and sometimes maintaining a stable equilibrium. In a human social system, its members and their learned behaviors are the stock that acts as a buffer against change until some new variable becomes a catalyst for an inalterable transformation in its stock and an evolution of the prevailing systems for living.

So in retrospect, the agricultural revolution that converted almost all successful hunter-gatherers to farmers 12,000 years ago was probably inevitable. A successful system of hunting and gathering tends to stabilize at no more than 250 members for any one nomadic group. This is because, if the population grows much larger than that, it tends to trigger a feedback loop communicating that a new system for staying alive will be less stressful and more effective—namely, staying put and settling down in one secure location with plentiful resources.

A feedback loop may cause the stock in any kind of system to maintain itself, grow, or diminish. Obviously, there can be any number of feedback loops within a complex system, feeding information back into the system that either helps it to change or to maintain its characteristic patterns over time. The primary stabilizing feedback loop that maintained hunting and gathering behavior was its success in keeping the group alive. Populations thus started to grow—whether through births or the banding together of successful groups of hunter-gatherers choosing to network and cooperate for survival with other clans rather than clash. Once too much growth had occurred, the very success of small and nimble hunting-gathering systems rendered them unsustainable.

The creation of effective farming systems for survival was a monumental shift in the collective intelligence of the human species. And the remarkable thing is that it didn't happen in just one place—the creation of agrarian systems for tilling the land happened in every place where hunting and gathering had already been successful. Rather than tracking wild game for meat, large herds of animals would be domesticated and shepherded. Rather than foraging for food sources and gathering what could be cut from the vine and carried away, large crops would be cultivated and maintained by a growing number of subsistence farmers. The widespread creation of agriculture was obviously common sense.

FROM SUBSISTENCE FARMING TO A SYSTEM OF EXCESS

Societies built around the food-producing behavior of subsistence farming became the dominant system for human survival for many thousands of years. But along with the creation of an agrarian culture and new farming techniques came other inventions now possible for social networks that no longer needed to relocate with regularity: the development of irrigation and food storage technologies; the building up of villages and towns and the means for fortifying and defending them from traveling marauders; nonportable art, architecture, and other permanently installed cultural artifacts; trade strategies with other villages and towns along with ever more complex social roles and divisions of labor.

So when did lifestyles of subsistence farming shift toward lifestyles producing excess and profit? It is important to note that the stock within a sedentary and agrarian social system is no longer just its populace, i.e., the numbers of people it is able to support and accumulate. Power itself may also be accumulated, through multiple means. It is noteworthy that human settlements were sitting targets—the population couldn't just pack up their tents and run away when danger was at the gates. Whoever could protect the rest of the individuals within a feudal social system accumulated power. Moreover, the individuals with the largest crops or herds also accumulated power. Those individuals with the most land to be farmed and grazed accumulated power. Those individuals with the most water or salt or manure or other needed resources on their land also accumulated power. Those individuals who accumulated the most tenant farmers and other laborers to look after their privateered property were also in a position to accumulate power.

TO CONTINUE THE ORIGIN STORY OF A CREATIVE social system based on the accumulation of capital, we must shift our overview to a location above what would eventually become Western Europe. Pre-Renaissance Europe was still organized in an agrarian social arrangement and had been settled as a network of feudal manors; each manor was a system for farming the landscape. The essence of the feudal social system was that accumulated power was maintained as a legal and political arrangement—power was displayed and maintained through the pageantry of inherited nobility and supported through obligatory labor, demonstrations of allegiance or *homage*, and sometimes even monetary contributions from the manor's tenant and peasant classes.

The manor worked as a mutually beneficial arrangement, including a *demesne*—a home farm that was the exclusive domain of the owner—and *alienated lands*, as they were called, farmed by tenants. The manorial system even maintained its own legal jurisdiction and court of law extending only to those either living on the manor or holding land there. The manorial lord offered peasants hereditary use of a portion of his estate for subsistence farming. In exchange for their work, the landlord offered protection. Landlords owned the means of production and the full rights to excess land yield.

Between 500 AD and 1086 AD, the population density of transalpine Europe expanded from about nine persons per square mile to thirty. At the same time, the feudal social arrangement and standard of living for peasants and serfs who tended to the agricultural activities of the typical manor remained fairly consistent. However, over the course of time and with social stability, the population eventually did begin to grow, once again altering the system of communal social relationships.

[A]s density [continued to rise], efficiency declined, and so did agricultural profitability from the point of view of both peasants and feudal lords. This encouraged the feudal lords to seek supplementary sources of income, the most important of which was the raising of sheep for wool, which in turn restricted the amount of land available for food crops, reduced the size of peasant holdings, pauperized much of the rural population, and stimulated migrations to the towns and wool production centers.[7]

Attempts were made to increase land yield by alternative methods from the use of fertilizer to crop rotation. Yet the effort to stretch the productiveness of arable land was unmatched by equivalent expansions of grazing pasture and animal quality necessary to provide plentiful manure. As a result, population growth outstripped food resources. Grain prices went up. The standard of living plummeted. Between 1310 and the 1340s there was a constant scarcity of food and, oftentimes, famine. Increasing malnourishment and migrations of populace, coupled with poor sanitation and denser living conditions provided a deadly combination of factors that reached a tipping point with the introduction of the pandemic of bubonic, pneumonic, septicemic, and enteric plagues when they arrived from Asia. The resulting event was known as the Black Death or The Great Mortality, which decimated European towns and villages.

The ongoing toll of the Plague upon the pre-Renaissance European social system was uncontrolled and would continue to wreak havoc in unexpected ways:

In the aftermath of the plague, Europe entered a period of intense economic unrest. The feudal kingdoms were shaken from top to bottom by massive peasant uprisings, messianic movements, an outbreak of cults that practiced self-flagellation, massacres of Jews, schisms within the Catholic Church, crusades to suppress heretics, the founding of the Inquisition, and a ceaseless round of wars, one of which is known appropriately as the Hundred Years War (1337–1453).[8]

It is important to remember that the medieval agrarian social system was dependent upon a rural peasantry that, even in the most urbanized regions of Europe, could comprise up to three quarters of the populace.[9] The feudal social system was already destabilized by the temptation of manorial landlords to grasp after greater income than could be yielded by typical tenant farming relationships. Thus, this system had already been in flux even before the fearsome Black Plague. Consequently, the incredible losses of tenant farming populace from the devastating pestilence only served to accelerate the disintegration of feudalism and the evolution of European society toward the greater security blanket of excess accumulation. Mercantilism emerged as a social behavior based on creating marketable goods and other kinds of desirable merchandise for profitable trading. Excess was good. This profit motive, based on the very real experience of extreme societal insecurity and loss, was a precursor to the development of free-market capitalism.

As the use of money became commonplace, more and more manorial lords chose to commute the customary dues and services owed by their tenant farmers, or vassals, and by their associated serfs, or agricultural laborers, into income-producing rental contracts more advantageous in a growing exchange economy. However, the plagues and wars had cut the rural population in half, and in some regions to barely a third of previous levels. Nor were local landlords themselves spared this calamity. Other powerful lords would eventually reclaim the devastated countryside, with some areas having been nearly abandoned. In time, trade began to flourish as never before as Europeans recovered to an increased focus on industry, enlightenment, and exploration. But the fear of the unknown and the need for more secure revenue streams continued to drive the post–Black Death breakdown of prior social affiliations; vassals and serfs were increasingly manumitted, and often evicted, in favor of hired labor. An agrarian social system no longer made economic sense in the midst of the greater mercantile opportunity of the mid-fifteenth to sixteenth centuries.

> Where the market was exclusively local, agriculture remained of necessity unspecialized and landlords preferred to rent out their whole estates to tenant farmers because this was the easiest way to ensure themselves a money income. Under these circumstances, the manorial lord became a rentier. Where landlords could grow wool or grain for export, they preferred to assert their absolute ownership of the estate and engage in capitalist agriculture, the rational exploitation of a large holding to produce a cash crop for commercial profit. Under these circumstances, the manorial lord became a capitalist farmer.[10]

The creation of social systems for profitable trading did not end with the production of wool products for the local mercantile economy. Starting around 1415, the Portuguese began their naval expeditions down what is known as the Gold Coast of Africa in search of a direct and usurping route to the gold trade stemming from the African kingdoms of Guinea. Their hope was to supplant hostile Moslems of the Sahara and the Maghrib in the control of that lucrative trade. Moreover, the Portuguese sought to cultivate Christian alliances in Ethiopia, and possibly India, against the perceived threat of the non-Christian infidel. So successful was their strategy of indirect collaborations with trading partners, so transforming was the wealth procured, that Portugal soon began the issuance of its first national gold coin, the *crusado*.

Alongside the gold that was acquired—or more accurately, plundered on the cheap from other lands and civilizations—there were also treasures like ivory, ebony, pearls, and melegueta pepper. And after the colonization of São Tomé off of Cameroon, cane sugar was added as a traded commodity, produced on estates worked by Negro slaves. In time, the Portuguese—with an increasing prowess in shipping, navigation, and gunnery—were able to turn the corner around the Cape of Good Hope, and focus their sights upon naval control of the profitable issuance of spices from Indian and Eastern Asia. Wildly prosperous yet again—this time on the trade of rare culinary enlivenments like camphor, cinnamon, nutmeg, ginger, cardamom, pepper, and cloves—by the year 1530, Portugal would turn also to the trade of African slaves. Portugal's behavior of trade acquisitions would trigger a swarm of slave ships departing Western Europe to support its nations' burgeoning annexations of profitable colonial territories.

The excesses of wealth generated by the trade and procurement of non-wage-earning labor was more than could have been imagined, and would soon attract the participation of Spain, France, and Great Britain. Even so, the profitability of colonialism would be taken to a whole new level by the discovery of the New World. "The Spanish looked first for an alternative and better route to the spices, pearls, and treasures of the Indies. They discovered instead a new world, but they found there gold and silver in hitherto unimagined quantities."[11]

Mining in the New World was made profitable because extraction was easily achieved by forcing large numbers of docile Indians into tacit slavery, dredging sand and gravel in streams. Eugene F. Rice, Jr. has defined industrial capitalism as the modern West's peculiar social system, the indirect collaboration of two distinct social networks—entrepreneurs, or capitalists, and wage earn-ers. The capitalist "owns and controls the capital invested in the business...owns the raw material...owns and markets the final product...owns the means of production."[12] On the other hand, in this arrangement the worker is now economically dependent, owning only his or her labor and selling that labor in exchange for wages. It is not difficult therefore to understand the allure of prac-ticing a variation on production wherein the capitalist adventurer also owns his or her laborers as personal property. The practice of human trafficking and slave-holding has always produced the same results—it continues to be enormously profitable to arrange labor for minimum wages.

SOCIAL CONSEQUENCES

It is crucial to understand that with the destruction and exploita-tion of other non-Western social systems, the sudden influx of wealth and resources triggered a feedback loop compounding the creative capacity and industrial invention of Western nations. The New World was exploited for all it was worth, on the one hand with native slave labor, and on the other hand with more durable African slave labor. It is documented for example that "[d]uring the sixteenth century...a flood of bullion poured into Europe...[shipments] mostly of gold—from Hispaniola, Cuba, Puerto Rico, and Central America."[13] In the 1540s, roughly 1.5 million ounces of silver per year was being shipped in; by the 1590s, over 10 million ounces each year. That was just the begin-ning of the accumulation of capital wealth from colonialism and the trade of merchandise and slaves that would eventually fund the Industrial Revolution.

But the swarm intelligence that produces creativity and invention can also produce a rampant contagion of self-serving ideological changes when we lose sight of the most complete overview. The one best hope for all humanity to thrive is for social systems to indirectly collaborate for mutual survival with neighboring social systems and cooperate with the pulse of surrounding ecosystems. Unfortunately, the West's initial encounter with the raw materials of the New World—the raw frontiers and climates, raw arable soils and spices, raw flora and seed crops, raw fauna and furs, and raw, dark-skinned, and largely naked laborers—adversely changed the way Western Europe thought of itself in relation to the rest of the world. Imperialistic, hierarchical and utterly racist justifications for its behavior toward other human beings and their social systems became the norm. As a result, neighboring societies were ravaged and lands privatized.

For example, Tzvetan Todorov estimates that during the years between 1500 and 1600, 70 million of the inhabitants of the Americas were exterminated by direct murder, cruel and indifferent treatment, and by the spread of European diseases. In Mexico alone, on the eve of its conquest, its population stood at approximately 25 million; in 1600 only 1 million native inhabitants remained alive.[14] Centuries later in America, at the very beginning of the American saga, Native Americans were declared to be savages, unfit to retain dominion over their own land. And in a 1787 Constitutional compromise, a slave was declared to be equal in measure only to three-fifths of a man in the determination of a Southern state's representation in the U.S. House of Representatives. Negroes, as African Americans were once called, were deemed unfit for citizenship or equal protections and privileges under the law. This latter belief continued to proliferate even after the Civil War:

> God created him a Negro—a different and inferior being, and there-fore, designed him for a different and inferior social position. Society, or the State, has ignored the work of the Almighty, and declared that he should occupy the same position and live out the life of the white man; and the result is, the laboring and producing classes are burdened with his support, and society, to a certain extent, poisoned by his pres-ence…it is absolutely certain that, as a class, they will become extinct, and a hundred years hence it is reasonable to suppose that no such social monstrosity as a "free negro" will be found in America.[15]

Ultimately, swarm intelligence is a double-edged sword. Just as it can produce free market economies and the most productive social, industrial, cultural, and political revolutions imaginable, it can also produce virulently and enduringly destructive social behaviors. Creativity is not a neutral concept. Creative acts can benefit the many, or they can benefit very few and harm the many.

A swarm theory of generative social behavior explains the emergence of collective creativity that is hyper-advantageous to one's particular hive, but it also explains the rapid spread of divisive and belittling ideologies and behaviors that are hyper-destructive to neighboring collectives. Heinous acts of inhumanity can be highly creative in their implementation of strategies for destroying other human swarms viewed as competitors, threats, or simply irrelevant. The history of human social relationships is replete with stories of smart swarms behaving together effec-tively, such as the women's suffrage and Civil Rights movements.

History is also rife with cognitive contagions such as racism and xenophobia. It all depends on one's overview.

In summary, behave like you're part of a social system—*reinforce and strengthen your most creative thinking with a positive feedback loop—your relationship with a circle of allies and friends.*

CHAPTER FOUR

SWARMS

COLLABORATIVE LEADERSHIP AND THE PROFESSIONAL IMAGINATION

A video went viral over YouTube late in 2011, showing two young ladies in a canoe as they encounter a massive cloud of starlings wheeling about over the River Shannon in Ireland. It is an amazing sight when a flock of thousands of birds suddenly changes direction at what appears to be exactly the same time. They are engaging in swarm intelligence, a phenomenon that is found in evidence across the animal world.

Swarm intelligence shapes the behavior of insect colonies, animal herds, schools of fish, bird flocks, and human communities alike. Serving as an advantage to the whole community and to the individuals that make up the whole, swarm intelligence is a different order of thinking than autonomic impulses or semi-conscious instincts. Like any intelligence, conscious choices are involved. But swarm intelligence is emergent, with choices distributed across the actions of multiple agents, as when a person swivels his gaze upward with a gasp and ducks in a crowd—only to be followed by everyone within a near radius stopping, spinning their heads, and ducking as well. These sudden shifts in the behavior of the surrounding community can be minor when measured one by one, and yet breathtakingly stunning as the responses spread in a domino effect.

The shape-shifting flock of starlings in the YouTube video, ebbing and flowing through the air at speeds of up to 20 miles per hour, is called a murmuration. I love the etymology of words but in this case, I like the connotations even better—murmurs of the heart, a stir of echoes, and the sensation of the pulse of the earth all come to mind when I repeat this word in my thoughts. Made up of a swarm of thousands of small winged organisms, each acting on the basis of its individual perceptions, the murmuration of starlings chased, separated, aligned, and converged again and again—behaving together as one self-organizing superorganism with a pattern of collaborative and interchanging leadership carrying them from point A, to point B, to the point just beyond.

THE FOUR LAWS OF SWARM BEHAVIOR

There are four laws governing the behavior of all swarms, whether biological, zoological, or human. These laws are interactive and always simultaneously at work, a system of interactions guiding any swarm's successful constitution and lasting impact upon the landscape. We may call them the Law of Succession, the Law of Separation, the Law of Alignment, and the Law of Cohesion. Each of these behavioral laws fosters *indirect collaboration* within a social network, a key principle of swarm intelligence and collective creative leadership.

The individual members of a swarm of social activity *chase* after those directly ahead of them, those temporarily blocking the path toward a role in the ranks of leadership; this chasing behavior steers each member toward taking over the position of those who have modeled a trajectory that leads to the front of the pack, ensuring a short-range succession of new leaders one right after another. Swarms behave in accordance with the Law of Succession to foster their own adaptability and forward momentum over time.

The individual members of a swarm of social activity each *separate* from those too close for comfort; this separating behavior steers each member clear of crowding their neighbors, ensuring a short-range repulsion of those who would otherwise inhibit that member from rotating forward into a leading position. Swarms behave in accordance with the Law of Separation to prevent a chain of disorienting or disabling collisions that would slow the progress of the group toward its next position.

The individual members of a swarm of social activity each *align* with those comfortably beside them; this aligning behavior steers each member toward the average heading of those keeping pace right alongside them, ensuring limits on the speed of a cohort of peers so that no member of the group gets left behind over the long haul. Swarms behave in accordance with the Law of Alignment to maintain enduring micro-attachments, tightly knit integral clusters that also preserve the fabric of the larger group.

The individual members of a swarm of social activity *cohere* with those around them, sticking together with the entire surrounding group; this cohesive behavior steers each member toward arriving at the destination of the multitude that surrounds them at just about the same time, ensuring the long-range convergence of the group upon some target. Swarms behave in accordance with the Law of Cohesion to prevent any member and his or her contribution to the group from getting lost or overlooked along the way.

In this chapter, I will review the phenomenon of swarm intelligence on display in some of the greatest business innovations of the twentieth century, each representing one of the laws of swarm behavior in action. I will also offer some speculations about how these laws, when taken together as a whole, offer a blueprint for further creative development in the arenas of culture, politics, economics, and education.

FROM SCENARIO PLANNING TO THE PERFORMANCE OF DEMOCRACY: EXAMPLES OF SWARM CHASING

The most creative and successful social institutions in recent history, whether they were profit-making or primarily charitable ventures, have all demonstrated a keen understanding of human behavior. But perhaps the most important understanding about human behavior is that for all of our complexity, we are basically social creatures—and social creatures follow very simple rules. These rules are the four laws of swarm behavior. On the human journey—both within swarms and across competing swarms of social behavior—individuals and the networks we bind ourselves together within will chase those in the lead, separate from those too close for comfort, align with those we are attempting to keep pace with, and cohere together in a targeted convergence with those headed in the same general direction.

Even though the outcomes of the interaction between swarms of human social behavior are emergent and impossible to predict with any certainty, it is very possible to predict a number of possible scenarios just ahead and to strategize how we might respond based on these four laws. In the early 1970s, Royal Dutch/Shell, a multinational oil and gas company, began investing in long-term strategic planning in part speculating on the possible behavior of a competing swarm of oil-producing nations known as the Organization of the Petroleum Exporting Countries (OPEC). Scenario analysis, as it was termed, was an adaptation of military swarm intelligence used to guide command decisions when facing an adversary. In other words, scenario analysis was a way of projecting ahead, chasing the leading edges of surrounding cloud of social activity. In the case of Shell, chasing the possible scenarios of OPEC behavior led to some advance creative problem solving:

> In one scenario, an accident in Saudi Arabia led to the severing of an oil pipeline, which in turn decreased supply. That created a market reaction that increased oil prices, allowing OPEC nations to pump less oil and make more money. The tale spooked [Shell's] executives enough to make them reexamine their assumptions about oil price and supply. Was OPEC preparing to increase oil prices? What would be the implications if they did? As a consequence, when OPEC announced its first oil embargo [in 1973], Shell handled the challenges better and faster than the competition. Within two years, Shell moved from being the world's eighth biggest oil company to being the second biggest.[1]

Shell's awareness of the Law of Succession and its own ability to chase down the OPEC cartel as those member nations aggressively took over the lead ultimately helped Shell to jockey to a position in the front ranks of all oil and gas producing companies.

CHASING AFTER A VISION OF DEMOCRACY IS another story altogether. In the aftermath of the tremendous fraud, loss, and lack of regulatory oversight that precipitated the global financial crisis of 2007–2008, the Great Recession that directly followed, the Occupy Wall Street movement, and other affiliated protests, I have begun to consider what it means to perform contemporary democracy. I recently joined a small community-based musical theater project in Syracuse called the "Dream Freedom Revival"; we are guided by the ethos that "democracy is driven by those who participate in it." It is easy to forget that participation in a democracy involves much more than standing on the sidelines, applauding as if it was a parade through our neighborhood—we must chase ahead after the vision and the work of those who have led the enactment of democracy long before you or I entered the struggle.

Whether we speak of the historical Abolitionist, woman's suffrage, and Civil Rights movements—or the more recent Arab Spring, and Occupy Together movements—there is a creative, narrative, and often counter-narrative arc to social movements, attempting either to tell an untold story, or to resist telling a story that falsely names, too neatly packages, or utterly obscures a life-sustaining truth. One of those inalienable truths is that identity is a work of art—and that the process of making identity is messy, especially within a democratic political context where so many contradicting ideas compete for our attention. Progressive movements are typified by swarms advocating for a more just society chasing ahead after the next possibility of democracy.

It is important to note that the difference between such progressive movements and those like the conservative Tea Party movement in the United States is the difference between chasing behavior and reactionary behavior—it is the difference between a creative swarm, struggling ahead toward greater mutual advantage, and the noisy clamor of "taking back" America to a point in its social development when an appalling number of its citizens were viewed as either totally invisible or totally insignificant.

The story of American identity is an ongoing performance. One thing stands out in the daily clamor—our identities are often shaped in opposition to what we most adamantly claim not to be. Accordingly, there are those who will only recognize the performance of conservatism as the mark of a great American, or assume that only liberals are able to act with open minds. In reality, every identity is a performance either of who we think we are in the world, or who we wish to be. Our competing claims about personal identity are as varied as the stories we tell of America, and every reinterpretation of America's possibilities has important consequences. Performances of collective, creative social action are as real as everyday life—every act of courage and vision, no matter how each act succeeds the next, is a duty performed out of the belief that our nation or loved ones stand in dire need of our contribution.

FROM SKUNK WORKS TO ART WORKS: EXAMPLES OF SWARM SEPARATION

No one seems to stand apart from the crowd more than the *Looney Tunes* cartoon character Pepé Le Pew. The malodorous presence of this amorous animated skunk has always been enough to drive others screaming in the opposite direction. However, the Law of Separation from those too close for comfort within human swarms is a response far more subtle than those who left behind billowing smoke trails in their frenzy to separate themselves from Pepé Le Pew.

In business history, the origin of the term "skunkworks" dates back to June 1943 and the research, design, and concept development of the experimental XP-80 jet fighter. Skunk Works was the official alias for the Advanced Development Programs of Lockheed Martin, an American aeronautics and aerospace, defense contracting, and advanced technology company. Originally set up to work in a closely guarded circus tent next to a plastics factory within the city of Burbank in southern California, the Lockheed research and development swarm associated the factory's foul smells wafting into their secret workspace with the fictional "Skonk Works" business venture as described in Al Capp's popular "Li'l Abner" comic strip. The story of the development of this experimental jet fighter exemplifies the speed that comes when a group of creative thinkers finds separation from the crowd:

> The Air Tactical Service Command (ATSC) of the Army Air Force met with Lockheed Aircraft Corporation to express its need for a jet fighter. A rapidly growing German jet threat gave Lockheed an opportunity to develop an airframe around the most powerful jet engine that the allied forces had access to, the British Goblin. Lockheed was chosen to develop the jet because of its past interest in jet development and its previous contracts with the Air Force. One month after the ATSC and Lockheed meeting, the young engineer Clarence L. "Kelly" Johnson and other associate engineers hand delivered the initial XP-80 proposal

to the ATSC. Two days later the go-ahead was given to Lockheed to start development and the Skunk Works was born, with Kelly Johnson at the helm.[2]

Amazingly, the prototype for the Lockheed P-80 Shooting Star was built and delivered in just 143 days from the start of the design process. Today, a *skunkworks* project is understood to be "one typically developed by a small and loosely structured group of people who research and develop a project primarily for the sake of radical innovation," innovation requiring the space to maneuver apart from the crowd.[3] Why was the delivery of this invention so rapid? Skunk Works represented an understanding of the Law of Separation in the arena of business industry; the Lockheed parent corporation allowed the smaller Skunk Works swarm of innovators enough advance funding and separation from bureaucratic interference to be as creative as it wanted to be as quickly as it needed to be.

Decades earlier, legendary General Motors CEO Alfred P. Sloan mastered an understanding of the Law of Separation in the arena of the consumer market. Realizing that consumers sought separation from their neighbors, and products that showed evidence of their upward mobility, Sloan pioneered the idea of "a car for every purse and purpose" with a pricing structure patterned after a ladder of success. Not only did Sloan price the Chevrolet, Pontiac, Oldsmobile, Buick, and Cadillac in an escalating tier from lowest to highest priced, he also created a segmentation within the structure of GM to cater to each swarm of consumers as if they were separate markets. The management teams for the design and production of each automobile were allowed the maneuvering room to operate as separate companies.

Such are the nuances of the Law of Separation through the lens of business and marketing innovation. But these nuances also exist in the arts and other creative professions. This separation of behaviors and practices allows for wide variation in multiple swarms of creative activity. The arts have long been a tool for recording knowledge about the human condition, but they are also a catalyst for human *development*, each art practice serving as a means of bearing fruit by capturing, organizing, and reinterpreting experiential data, both individual and cultural, *about* the human experience. Thus, it is necessary to attain a clearer conception of the various systems for defining, teaching and creating new ideas within the arts and design professions, so as to rethink how these strategies might be utilized in jumpstarting American innovation.

Art can be defined and understood through three very separate models. The models are so different it is not uncommon for practitioners of any one approach to art-making to view works of art and design produced by the other approaches as if they were skunking up the art world. One model defines art as *a system of production*, a cause and effect intervention resulting in a stockpile of manipulated natural and manufactured materials, with a focus on technical mastery "that has as its basic intent a cognitive interest in the control of objects in the world."[4] Within this model, arts and design practices seek to produce precious objects, forms, and movements using techniques to shape their beauty and aesthetics as validated by the arbiters of good taste.[5] An example may be seen in the oil paintings of the High Renaissance Masters collected at The Metropolitan Museum of Art or a dance performance at the Kennedy Center.

The arts and design professions defined as a system of production are *formational*—giving form to ideas borne in mind.

Viewing the arts as a system of production invites collaboration with other creative swarms that teach individuals to give form to ideas through a physically manifested medium or material. Those with an affinity for technically rigorous, carefully observed creative practices that generate beautiful forms, structures, and masterfully singular solutions will likely find a practical kinship with industrial and interactive designers, with architects, poets, filmmakers, and scientists. Successful ventures in this category include the elegant consumer electronics and personal computers of Apple or the soaring architecture of Frank Gehry.

Another model defines art as *a system of communication*, the expression of situated knowledge about a person's relationship with his or her social world.[6] Arts and design practices within this model express and reinterpret "the ways in which we immediately experience an intimacy with the living world, attending to its myriad textures, sounds, flavors, and gestures" through selected artistic media.[7] An example may be seen in the body art of the Maori people, with meanings that are permanently etched and yet as transitory as the human flesh it is tattooed upon.

The arts and design professions defined as a system of communication are *informational*—further informing ideas and practices developing in mind. Viewing the arts as a system of communication invites collaboration with other creative swarms that teach individuals to think expressively in a language. Those with an affinity for interpretive creative practices that navigate the signs and symbols humans shape in order to convey valued signifiers will likely find a practical kinship with writers of all kinds, mathematicians, musicians, dancers, and a multicultural array of ethnic, religious, and social communities. Successful ventures in this category include the entire song catalog of The Beatles or the film studios and entertainment properties of The Walt Disney Company.

A third model defines art as *a system of social critique*, a form of intervention and activism rendering invisible assumptions, values, and norms visible "in order to transform" and critique unjust social relations and empower marginalized individuals and communities.[8] Arts and design practices within this model challenge "taken-for-granted theories and concepts that govern our disciplines and circumscribe our thinking" in order to reveal "the ongoing inequity and social injustice that shape our society."[9] An example may be seen in the large body of diverse works of art created during the Harlem Renaissance, shattering destructive stereotypes of the African American identity.

The arts and design professions defined as a system of social critique are *transformational*—reflecting upon and critiquing ideas, practices, and relations that have become overly fixed in mind and too easily accepted as given. Viewing the arts as a system of social critique invites collaboration with other creative swarms that teach individuals to question their contexts, confront injustice, and to traverse the gaps in assumed knowledge. Those with an affinity for critical creative practices that question situated or embodied contexts will likely find practical kinship with feminists, iconoclasts, revolutionaries, cultural theorists, mass media dissenters, political activists, and environmentalists. Successful ventures in this category include the popular culture influences of the early twentieth century Harlem Renaissance and contemporary hip hop culture or social/environmental activism reflected in works of street art and community theater across the globe.

Separating from the crowd allows for a more nimble and adaptable approach to creation of works of art and design, one that transcends competition between these three different models of aesthetic problem solving, creating opportunities for varying social swarms to become adept at playing across the unnecessary boundaries separating product-consumer, expressive-communicative, and critical-activist professional arts and design activities.

FROM THE ASSEMBLY LINE TO AFRICAN AMERICAN IDENTITY: EXAMPLES OF SWARM ALIGNMENT

In the automobile industry, the innovations of Henry Ford preceded those of Alfred P. Sloan. Henry Ford's concept of the assembly line for the production of his Model T automobiles was actually three innovations—one mechanical, one involving labor management, and the last involving consumer behavior. The mechanical innovation involved marrying two other successful production inventions from two other unrelated fields of thought and industry: George Eastman's strategy for the assembly of standardized photography equipment using carefully refined and easily interchangeable parts that could be fitted within any completed product, and the strategy employed at Chicago meat-packing houses for bringing the work to a laborer's station rather than having laborers move about and eventually find their way to the next work task.

Ford had personally observed pulley systems and a converted grain mill conveyor belt bringing carcasses to workers at fixed stations to be butchered. Ford reverse conceptualized the use of the very same dynamics—not to butcher and remove smaller cuts from a single slab of meat—but employed in the assembly of a single product, all in one continuous, carefully aligned flow. Those dynamics required an economy of motion from the laborer, never moving from his workstation. This further entailed a principled adherence to a strict division of labor, breaking up the assembly of the Model T into 84 distinct steps wherein each worker was trained to do a single step.

But this was mind-numbing and boring work. For this reason, Ford chose to build in some incentives for the laborer to do it—this was Ford's second great innovation. So in 1913, the first assembly line in large-scale manufacturing was up and running and by 1914 the laborers on that line received pay raises so comparatively high that other industrialists branded Ford as a "traitor to his class." This and other incentives made it easier for employees to become potential consumers of their own labor and purchase their own Model Ts with the wages they had earned. Consequently, worker productivity increased—right along with the workers' pride in their collective handiwork, parked in front of their own homes.

Ford's ultimate aim was to capture the widest possible market share in an era when cars were typically expensive and custom made. In 1907 when he announced his vision for the Ford Motor Company to build "a motor car for the great multitude," Ford envisioned the sturdy Model T, an automobile with no factory options, not even a choice of color; this made it one of the least expensive cars available. Assembly line production efficiency and a lack of wasted effort made the Model T even cheaper still. Ford's third great innovation was to pass the savings on to the consumer. Ford famously said, "Every time I reduce the price of the car by one dollar I get one thousand new buyers," and the more automobiles he sold, the more he dropped the price of his Model T. In so doing, Ford aligned the market forces to favor his product and quickly became the leading car manufacturer in the world.

The creative achievement of Henry Ford and his team of production managers was in their innate understanding that human beings, like all social creatures, are inclined toward the Law of Alignment within swarms. In retrospect, Ford's innovations were in aligning the functions of his factory floor machinery toward one integrated set of manufacturing targets, massaging the behavior of his workers to embrace common production goals and a shared sense of compensatory reward, and in influencing the response of the consumer market in anticipation of his uniquely affordable inventory.

This collective creative achievement has been replicated in the business world since the time of Henry Ford. In the early 1930s, Procter & Gamble moved to decentralize its decision making and allow its Camay and Ivory soap brands to increase their success by realigning personnel into separate internal management teams, each making independent decisions that were nevertheless in full accord with the mission and vision of the larger corporation.

Procter & Gamble continues to lead the way in its understanding of the law of alignment within and across converging swarms of business activity, having launched the Connect + Develop program in the early 2000s, dedicated to the fostering of what is called "open innovation." Connect + Develop represents an open invitation for external innovators from anywhere in the world to share the breakthrough ideas they have developed in their own creative swarms and link them directly with Procter & Gamble's top company needs. To date, this alignment initiative has developed more than 2,000 global partnerships, and counting.

FOR CENTURIES, IT WAS ALMOST IMPOSSIBLE for most U.S. citizens to even to consider anyone of African descent as a fellow

American. In her book, *Making Whiteness: The Culture of Segregation in the South, 1890–1940*, author Grace Elizabeth Hale argues that the racializing of the American identity is a product of the post-Reconstruction South's deep need for stories and images pronouncing Black inferiority, a social reaction born of fear of the consequences of Black political and economic equality. The stigma of darkness—displayed on product advertisements, documented in studies and writings concluding a pathology of Black folk, collected in anthropometric statistical data "scientifically" proving the physical and mental inferiority of colored peoples, and made spectacle of in public events ranging from minstrel shows to lynchings—these were the stories and images propelled throughout the post–Civil War American consciousness.

These stories and images were circulated via a new consumer culture and growing common access to magazines and other publications, lithographs, and photographs (later, through radio, motion pictures, and television) as afforded by the industrial revolution. Race-based stories of identity "were made and marked at a time when technological change made the cheap production of visual imagery possible and the development of a mass market provided a financial incentive—selling through advertising—to circulate the imagery"[10]

In an 1874 *Harper's Weekly* political cartoon by Thomas Nast titled "Colored Rule in a Reconstructed (?) State," the caption reads "You are Aping the lowest Whites. If you disgrace your Race in this way you had better take Back Seats." In the cartoon, White legislators look on in the background with disdain and bemusement as caricatures of African Americans shake their fists and shout insults at one another, accomplishing nothing of significance. Stories are interactive episodes of the human experience—a way of narrating the world—and in this particular cartoon, recently emancipated African Americans were presented as social monstrosities and misfits. On display is the fear of the reinterpretation of American social relations gone awry, a narrative of civilization devolved into nonsense, with all legislation at a standstill while ugly and ill-suited African American politicians rail at one another.

> In 1863, the enslaved Americans were emancipated whereby they temporarily joined the ranks of the nation's free citizens at the very moment that public educational systems were being developed into their modern form. For a brief period during the late 1860s and 1870s, as free laborers, citizens, and voters, the ex-slaves entered into a new social system of capitalism, Republican government, and wage labor. Their campaign for first-class citizenship, however, was successfully undermined by federal and state governments and by extralegal organizations and tactics. Soon after the late 1870s, blacks were ruthlessly disenfranchised; their civil and political subordination was fixed in southern law, and they were trapped by statutes and social customs in an agricultural economy that rested heavily on coercive control and allocation of labor…they remained an oppressed people.[11]

In the decades thereafter, the idea of paying for "extravagant schoolhouses for the education of Negroes" with the tax revenues of White citizens was vehemently ridiculed.[12] The prevailing definition of the utter abnormality an ex-slave was that declaimed by Samuel Chapman Armstrong, who founded the Hampton Normal and Agricultural Institute in 1868 for the manual training of colored people. Chapman was of the opinion that his charges were mentally, morally, and materially destitute, each one burdened with the misfortune of character defects born of "[h]is low ideas of life and duty, his weak conscience, his want of energy and thrift," and "his indolent, sensuous tropical blood."[13]

The Hampton model of industrial training would become a seminal model in the education of colored folk, providing instruction in subaltern vocations such as farming (as in share-cropping), blacksmithing, shoemaking, and harness repair, and for girls, in the mending and making of clothing, washing, iron-ing, and cooking. This prescription for the appropriate education of Negroes was also explicated by John Dollard in his study of a Southern town in the 1930s where schools were used "to educate the Negro in order to fit him for place first as a slave and then as a caste man in society," an educational trajectory that would "prepare him for, but not beyond, the opportunities of lower-class status."[14]

Against this backdrop of a centuries-old Western story arc about those of African descent conveyed through visual imagery and cultural stereotypes that told only of ugliness and unaccept-ability in the world, how did African Americans manage to align ourselves as equal citizens in the United States? In a nation that made a practice of building physical, rhetorical, and legislative walls to keep people who look like me at the back of the line, how did Blacks move so comfortably beside our non-Black neighbors that one of us was unexpectedly elected President of the United States in 2008 and again in 2012?

This massive realignment of social identity was initiated through the visual art, design, literature, music, drama, and dance that emerged during the Harlem Renaissance as much as it was anyplace else.[15] In a May 10, 2007, *New York Times* website mul-timedia presentation about a new exhibition at the Schomburg

Center for Research in Black Culture in Harlem called "Stereotypes vs. Humantypes," images featuring Blacks in the nineteenth and twentieth centuries were displayed revealing how widespread stereotyped and distorted representations of Blacks were during that time period, and how African Americans visually contested those distortions by simply documenting their everyday lives.[16]

This movement from segregation to mutual citizenry was facilitated by the insertion of a visual argument and new performance of identity within the public consciousness. The discourse of race, ethnicity, and cultural difference typically boils down to a visual argument. Historically, the evidence of race has been the flesh, hair, and skull—the raw data in which difference is first perceived. But the evidence of ethnic and cultural difference also tends to be based in artifacts and accoutrements of language and everyday living. Wherever difference is perceived, this kind of raw data has also typically been implicit in the indictment that one subgroup of humanity is uglier, less intelligent, and more inferior than another.

In the early twentieth century, most African Americans were so disenfranchised they were rendered invisible in their contributions to society unless given a platform by wealthy patrons, through social welfare or special government work programs, or by liberal-minded and philanthropic White society. The visual representation of the African American body in Western visual culture—in commercial advertisement, paintings, popular souvenir postcards, etc.—has featured the relentless effort of those who sought to define us as either less than human, less than American, less than Christian, or less than statistically significant. African American identity was essentially reduced to a framing definition against which one could contradistinguish Whiteness.

John Henry Adams, Jr. was one of the first to write of the African American as a beautiful creation of God, aligned with the beauty depicted in classical Western works of art: "Here is the real new Negro man. Tall, erect, commanding, with a face as strong and expressive as Angelo's Moses and yet every whit as pleasing and handsome as Rubens's favorite model. There is that penetrative eye about which Charles Lamb wrote with such deep admiration, that broad forehead and firm chin...."[17]

But the inauguration of the performance and presentation of the "New Negro" throughout the Harlem Renaissance from the 1920s to the mid-1930s was an incomplete response to the visual argument of racial inferiority, merely a first attempt at changing the way the raw data had been weighted against us. It did not go far enough to subvert the warrant for the argument that we were, are, and have always been an ugly people. Deborah Willis makes the point that "[t]he architects of the 'New Negro' doctrine could not, quite naturally, [fully] define the African-American experience through [the dominant culture caricatures], so there was a concerted effort to find the 'self' in visual images."[18]

As part of a 2006 research grant I had won while I was on faculty at Penn State University, I went on a search to find tangible evidence of the grassroots effort to realign African American identity in social, historical, and scholarly visual arguments. My initial goal was to travel to various Historically Black Colleges and Universities (HBCUs) to sketch and draw works and artifacts from their historical art collections, as well as to record written and sketched impressions of the people and places I interacted with along the way in autobiographical and testimonial fashion. If there was any physical evidence of the definitive "New Negro," were they not sure to be found in these collections of art by "New Negroes" as they were becoming new?

As I roamed through the Hampton University Museum, sketchbook in hand, I was halted in mid-step by a work of the artist Felrath Hines, entirely in black and white and full of geometrics. Hines was a member of *Spiral*, a group of about fifteen or so New York City–based artists of African American descent including Romare Bearden, Hale Woodruff, Charles Alston, Norman Lewis, and Richard Mayhew. Formed in 1963, the year of my birth, *Spiral* sought to explore race, identity, art, and the possible roles they might play in the Civil Rights movement in the era when Black would first be heralded in the United States as beautiful. A website relates the following exchange:

> Spiral member Norman Lewis framed the question: "Is there a Negro Image?" To which group member Felrath Hines responded, "There is no Negro Image in the twentieth century—in the 1960s. There are only prevailing ideas that influence everyone all over the world, to which the Negro has been, and is, contributing. Each person paints out of the life he lives."[19]

Several works by these artists were on display at the Hampton University Museum, such as Richard Mayhew's gorgeous *September*, a landscape painting. I was also struck by the work of Dr. Samella S. Lewis, including a painting called *Waterboy*; completed when she was a student at Hampton Institute, and yet here they were, still, in the museum's collection. And I was absolutely astounded by a series of serigraph, or silkscreen, prints by Jacob Lawrence titled *Hiroshima* featuring the manipulation of a single color palette of about four colors into eight wholly distinct color worlds and narrative episodes.

Inexorably, the "New Negro" was itself reinterpreted into the concept that "Black is beautiful." Whereas the "New Negro" remains a historical artifact, largely definitive in its initial introduction, the effort to draw upon and paint from the heart of the life one lives—out of localized conceptions of beauty and identity—has proven to be an inherently *emergent* exercise. "Black [as] beautiful" reinterprets African American identity a thousand instances a day, introducing an identity ever in flux into the visual culture and the lexicon of contemporary culture. But the reinterpretive bridge between the "New Negro" and "Black [as] beautiful" was to first see "Black as normal." "Black as normal" was revealed in thousands of professional studio photographs, Kodak snapshots, and art photography reproductions hung on walls, stuffed in shoeboxes on closet shelves, pasted into photo albums—and often even making their way to museum and gallery collections.

These photos were yet another method of the realignment that Alain Locke described in bodily measure as "the shaking off [of] the psychology of imitation and implied inferiority" and the "shedding of the old chrysalis" in the achievement of spiritual emancipation and self-understanding.[20] In so doing, the identity of people of African descent was brought into alignment with the American identity and the *African American* identity was made visible.

FROM SIX SIGMA TO DESIGN THINKING: EXAMPLES OF SWARM COHESION

I remember when the advent of more sophisticated computer graphics technology and complex algorithmic modeling made it possible to convincingly render a stampede of swarming wilde-beests in the 1994 Oscar-winning film *The Lion King*. In other words, there is no inherent disconnect between the mathematics of statistical models and the living work of art that a swarm can appear to be to the eye of the beholder. Six Sigma is such a statistical model, referring to quality control manufacturing processes able to produce a very high proportion of output over a short period of time within a specification of "six sigma quality," which translates numerically to long-term defect levels below 3.4 defects per million opportunities.

Although first developed by the Motorola telecommunications company, Six Sigma became famous in the 1990s when instituted by Jack Welch at the General Electric Corporation. In order to successfully converge upon this numerical target, the individual members of a business unit and production team had to cohere around a shared commitment to "making decisions on the basis of verifiable data and statistical methods, rather than assumptions and guesswork," especially from top-level management.[21]

IN 2009, EMILY PILLOTON WROTE A BOOK titled *Design Revolution: 100 Products That Empower People*, detailing 100 design products that empower people who are typically overlooked by commercial, for-profit designers. Pilloton's book highlights a swarm of thinkers converging upon something very different than a numerical target. She presents a vital challenge for the new century: how can creative professionals employ their arts and design practices to make a significant contribution regarding life and death matters such as the development of potable water supplies, the proliferation and preparation of food stocks, the conservation and development of energy systems, transportation concepts, and the production of affordable and easily accessible health and safety products? What social enterprise and entrepreneurship ideas might permanently turn the tide of global poverty? Pilloton argues for an increased convergence of business concerns and private advocacy on the beneficiaries of socially responsible design, "driven by a more humanitarian notion of service" wherein "the designer works to provide a useful, useable, and desirable product to those who are largely ignored by the market." Creative practices that focus on serving those in the global consumer market who are typically ignored and perpetually devalued help all of us to cohere around a common cause—preventing other human beings from being forever lost or overlooked along the way to a more just network of societies.

Design is a practice that involves the modeling of new approaches for everyday living. Both the arts and the sciences converge in the making of conceptual models, and it is very possible for a design to be derived as a hybrid of both arts-based and science-based inquiry. The 100 designs in Pilloton's *Design Revolution* are also models of *social entrepreneurship*, defined as locating a problem in society—i.e., circumstances and behaviors that are stuck, ineffective, or not working to empower people—and addressing that problem by introducing some kind of transformation into the system that first produced the problem, while persuading others to support that transformation.[22] Social entrepreneurship and responsible design principles flow from a critical-activist social behavior, which interrogates contemporary human circumstances and social contexts in continual acts of appraisal, agitation, and action.

It is hard to imagine any more compelling solutions to human social problems and to the changes we have caused to our global environment and infrastructure than those engaged daily by creative and socially responsible designers. These designs, and other solutions like them, promise the kinds of social improvements we would all do well to converge upon.

THE BIG PICTURE

Once we open our eyes to the fact that all human social behavior is swarm behavior, we can get smarter about identifying and fostering what comes naturally in all arenas of social activity, from business, to education, to community organizing. Whether we seek the greater development of an individual mind or the greater development of a nation, swarms change everything. When asked to reflect upon the mobilization of the Montgomery Bus Boycott that followed her refusal to move to the back of a bus on December 1, 1955, in segregated Alabama, Rosa Parks said, *"At the time I was arrested, I had no idea it would turn into this. It was just a day like any other day. The only thing that made it significant was that the masses of the people joined in."*[23] The swarm of community members turned activists that quickly filled in behind her changed the American social landscape.

Children figure out how to live and swarm creatively before they even enter a kindergarten classroom. Let's consider the hypothetical situation of two children at play. When little Sharon and Jason play a game together, Sharon teaches Jason *how to read* the rules and James, in turn, uses that knowledge *to make up new rules* that he then shares with Sharon. Then—whether chasing, separating, aligning, or converging—the swarm fills in behind them. In an art classroom that encourages innovation and creativity, the assignment might be to craft from wood scraps a human or animal figure that can stand on its own. The teacher allows Sharon and Jason to *read* each other's faulty starts and tentative successes as they figure out for themselves what pieces fit together and what shape their figure is taking, rather than giving them step-by-step "insert this here, connect that there" instructions. This is the most effective way to learn: fully engaged in a task at hand and situated within a small swarm of thinkers and doers, each learner making sense of prior knowledge, mimicking one another in order to solve a problem, and adapting new ways of knowing and doing.

America's system of public education and its recent preoccupation with high-stakes tests of individual learning achievement is missing the big picture and thereby failing our youngsters. Coaching students to pass individual achievement tests is not a catalyst for creativity. Rather, allowing students to swarm together in collaborative learning relationships is the key to stemming the ongoing mediocrity of public education. Our arts, design, and humanities classrooms are perhaps the first, best frontier available to establish a new vision for learning that truly leaves no child behind. Creating the means for more compromise and collaboration is the blueprint for a combative political climate that has lost its bearings and has stopped creating solutions.

The sobering understanding that we now live in an inextricably global economy is the only thing that has pulled our nations back from the brink of near worldwide financial disaster in 2008. But we must go further if we are to truly address the inequities of wealth that are continuing to trap entire nations in third-world squalor. More of the big picture will be addressed in the following chapter. Fortunately, the good news is that the idea of swarm intelligence has all the potential to spread like a feeding frenzy across borders and cultures. That's just the way that swarms function.

In summary, behave like you're part of a swarm—*chase ahead, separate from the crowd, align with the pacesetters, and converge upon a goal that benefits one and all.*

CHAPTER FIVE

SUPERORGANISMS

SOCIAL RESPONSIBILITY AND THE CIVIC IMAGINATION

There is a scene near the end of the popular Disney film *Finding Nemo* where Dory, a regal tang that has been a friend and companion to a clownfish named Marlin as he searches for his lost son Nemo, finds herself trapped in a deep-sea fishing net trawling for schools of grouper. As the heavy net is slowly cranked up toward the surface loaded with hundreds of thrashing fish, little Nemo bravely enters through an opening in the netting. In a flash of creativity in the midst of the swarm, Nemo convinces the doomed mass of fish that it is to their mutual advantage to all begin to swim down toward the ocean floor at the same time. Alone, no one grouper is very intelligent. But acting as one, they became for a time a *superorganism*, generating enough collective force of awareness, action, and momentum to snap the net from the boat and burst free. Working in concert, they brilliantly engineered their own great escape.

Likewise, swarm intelligence is manifested as a complex social behavior, an aggregate of individual agents each acting on the basis of local perceptions of the world they live in and trading positions in a carousel of self-similar behavior. Acting and responding as one, ordinary creatures can become more than themselves—for a time, the ordinary becomes extraordinary.

A FOURTH MAJOR PRINCIPLE OF SWARM intelligence is *adaptive mimicking* within a social network. Adaptive mimicking is an exponential force, distributed over a wide number of individual agents. "Superorganisms...exhibit a form of 'distributed intelligence,' a system in which many individual agents with limited intelligence and information are able to pool resources to accomplish a goal beyond the capabilities of the individuals."[1]

The basis for the emergence and functioning of any superorganism is a fundamental cooperation between organisms. Cooperation within any social swarm has a cumulative effect. So what happens when individuals stop cooperating? What happens when the accumulation of human knowledge and practice is disrupted, when the means of distributing intelligence is shattered, and the awareness is entirely lost to us that we must mimic one another to adapt in order to survive? How are we to engineer our own great escape?

In the absence of the widespread awareness and free exercise of swarm intelligence in addressing our most nagging social problems, human beings have become accustomed to living with voids and disconnects. Approximately 150,000 people die across the globe every day. But only about 100,000 of those people die every day from aging or natural causes.[2] The remaining deaths are devastating—they represent disruptions to the planet's social networks, a precipitous drain of its replenishing systems, a sudden diminishment to the numerical strength of its swarms. The loss of an individual is also the loss of a force to be reckoned with.

Not surprisingly, the needless loss of individual souls and their contribution to the overall functioning of society can absolutely incapacitate the ability to adaptively mimic. Similarly, the willful refusal to acknowledge that there is anything worth mimicking in those we choose to oppose—a behavior most immediately evident in contemporary political rhetoric and gamesmanship—accomplishes the very same dysfunction and social paralysis. As a result, voids and disconnects are left in place of our effectiveness at adaptively mimicking one another. Voids are left when people die from treatable diseases, preventable infections and contagions, homicide, suicide, accidents, the skirmishes of war, genocide, malnutrition, contaminated water and environmental disasters. It could be argued that humanity sustains itself with unexpected births offsetting unexpected deaths. But we hurt ourselves in other ways. Disconnects are created when new (often violent) factions are incited by divisive, self-aggrandizing individuals—or are suddenly detonated when the tinder of real or imagined insults and grievances are ignited by the flint and steel of contemporary tribal behavior. Human beings also generate the voids and disconnects that short circuit opportunities to behave as a superorganism when we work against the four laws that govern all swarm behavior.

We ultimately work against the best interests of the groups we identify with as well as the increase of our own personal capacities when we resist the Law of Succession. Instead of chasing after those directly ahead and allowing others the space to do the same, human beings too often work to capture leadership for themselves and permanently block others in their pathway forward. This obstructive behavior steers others toward invisibility since no one has eyes in back of his or her head or cares much about what is happening at the rear. However, sending others to the back of the bus—out of sight, out of mind—is a recipe for constructing social divisions, unchanging hierarchies, class resentments, and ensuring a more combative society. South Africa's history of apartheid and its continuing legacy is an example of resistance to the Law of Succession.

We hurt ourselves when we pervert the Law of Separation. Instead of separating from those too close for comfort while maintaining a healthy detachment that allows for independent choices, we fall into destructive patterns of excessive groupthink. We either become the enraged mob or vicious gang that sees diversity and those who look or think or behave differently as a thing to be destroyed—or we become the cult so obsessed with the power of its leader over their lives that it completely severs all meaningful attachments with those who look or think or behave otherwise. This homogenizing behavior steers those perceived as threats directly into so many disorienting or disabling collisions that mutually beneficial forward momentum becomes impossible, ensuring the congestive failure of the human superorganism as it attempts to function. North Korea, with its angry isolationist bombast and cult-like performances of blind devotion to its leaders, has fully emerged as a present-day example of the perversion of the Law of Separation.

We hurt ourselves when we disrupt the Law of Alignment. Instead of aligning shoulder to shoulder in deeply knit clusters, both learning and solving problems together, we tolerate misalignments that keep some groups permanently behind the rest; we solidify hierarchies in social, economic, and educational status; and we maintain corridors of daily living that allow those in privileged positions to gather advantages at breakneck speed without any true awareness of the daily plight of those who have been left behind. This complacent behavior ensures an unwillingness or inability to seek the common good above all, asserting instead the primacy of the individual and his private property or concerns. Seeking the common good above all does not require a socialist economic system. Nor does it require a capitalist economic system. It only requires a swarm intelligence that allows neighboring communities living in very different political and economic systems the grace to come alongside without fear of being demonized, oppressed, or torn asunder. The cycle of poverty and disorder in Third World nations left behind in the wake of hundreds of years of Western colonialism and wealth creation is still the best example of how disrupting the Law of Alignment continues to hurt us all.

We hurt ourselves when we defy the Law of Cohesion. Instead of the members of a swarm of social practice or ideology cohering with those around them, figuring out what it means to be human together, we purposely nudge the next guy's rear wheel to send our neighbor careening into the wall or off the track. This calculated zero-sum behavior is based on the belief that the other person's loss is likely to be my gain. But laying landmines and booby traps for one another only ensures a perpetual state of stalemate and a mutual inability to move forward toward an agreed-upon target. The lack of productivity that permeates the United States Capitol building in 2013 tells the disastrous tale of what happens to effective government when those elected to serve the nation become consumed with a refusal to compromise or give and take, defying the Law of Cohesion.

The remainder of this chapter presents a series of carefully considered proposals, intended to provoke the exercise of our civic imagination. If we assume there is still time to adapt our dysfunctional global society to a state of being much more akin to that of the human superorganism, what beneficial behaviors might we mimic? There is a reason why humanity remains obsessed with tales of superheroes and mythological demigods. We know we were meant to be much more than we are. It is in our social DNA.

Naturally, my proposals are based upon my experiences in the arts and design practices and education. I don't own these ideas (especially since I am sharing them freely) and I certainly cannot enact them on my own. Ideas belong to all of us. May they bear much fruit.

SWARM INTELLIGENCE PROPOSAL #1—THE BLACK BOX INITIATIVE

The erroneous perception that works of art can be summed up as static, inert, collectible, and aesthetically rendered objects of fancy has prompted arts advocates like Elliot W. Eisner to marshal all the arguments at their disposal in countering the resulting policy-making notion that the arts are "nice but not necessary."[3] Still, such policies persist. Current "Race to the Top" federal policy has done little to displace the prevalence of standardized testing strategies that came into favor in response to the No Child Left Behind Act. And there continues to be a "demoralized" climate suffered by arts educators in contexts where it is less and less expedient to support instruction for any activity in which there are no tests supposedly assuring both that students are learning something and that teachers are teaching something.[4]

But what if public policy was based instead on the idea of the arts as information? In his article "Art Education for New Times," Paul Duncum defines and describes the cultural ramifications of the Information Age. The Information Age was that period over the last quarter of the twentieth century that saw the rapid globalization of information and communication technologies and the proliferation of the ability to digitize and manipulate information and its traffic. The cultural developments of these new times include: "the treatment of culture as an ordinary, material commodity; the proliferation of electronic visual images; and, the multifaceted construction of individual identity."[5] The social effects of this YouTube-like glut of data have been described as follows:

> Human beings now produce more than [5 trillion megabytes] worth of recorded information per year: documents, e-mail messages, television shows, radio broadcasts, Web pages, medical records, spreadsheets, presentations, books…That is 50,000 times the number of words stored in the Library of Congress, or more than the total number of words ever spoken by human beings. Seventy-five percent of that information is digital…As the proliferation of digital media accelerates, we are witnessing profound social, cultural, and political transformations whose long-term outcome we cannot begin to foresee.[6]

The information often seems overwhelming. However, if we understand that the arts themselves have *always* been information, it allows us to adapt to this Information Age paradigm shift in unique ways. For ages, the arts have been an organizing system of the most human information of all—data impressed with responses to social need and packed with emotional meaning. The information we wring from and meld into manufactured forms, cultural symbols, and "let's-change-the-world" aesthetic treatises are rich piles of data stored up for a subsequent generation of the human race to reinterpret. Oral, visual, written and performance arts practices have long been adept at depicting heroes and monsters, gods and earth mothers, migrations and holy men, elements and alchemies, the sciences and religions, social injustices and fragile ecologies. Taken together, the various arts and design practices constitute some of the most dynamic strategies at our disposal for conserving and recycling the data that most effectively informs human beings of who we are, where we come from, what our purpose is, and where we may be going.

As a result of my awareness of the arts as information, I have begun to wonder what would happen if the arts and design in education adaptively mimicked the paradigm shifts of the Information Age.[7] Toward that end, I initiated a brief correspondence in 2007 with Dr. Nicholas Negroponte of MIT, the visionary behind the One Laptop per Child (OLPC) Initiative, a nonprofit organization offering inexpensive laptops for children in developing countries.[8] I forwarded a 10-point proposal that I believed would augment the OLPC Initiative by introducing a powerful intersection between OLPC, new technology, the Information Society, and the arts.

I wrote acknowledging the elegance of this initiative in seeking to provide access to one laptop per child in address of the chronic global crisis of inadequate education. I suggested that the success of the OLPC initiative must be unequivocally documented in order to protect the endeavor from its list of detractors. To do this, I argued that the OLPC Foundation needed to gather information from each child on the newfound significance of the laptop in their own lives, in their families, and in their communities.

I then pointed out that art-making yields a form of information native to the young—stories. Stories are data gathering, communication, and documentation all at once. In that sense, scientific technology, the "information society," and the arts are not far removed. They are parallel and often intersecting pathways to the same goals: the growth and development of the human species in its capacity to render the extraordinary out of the ordinary materials and events that constitute our lives, even in impoverished or war-torn areas of the world. If we simply shift our understanding of the arts in accord with the seismic social shifts that have resulted in the "information society," the practice of the arts will be recognized once again for what it is, an access point to learning. Those children with a learned facility for gathering data, generating empathy and understanding through effective communication, and documenting the significant events of our time for posterity, will ultimately catapult themselves to roles of vital importance in an information economy.

To accomplish this, I suggested that in addition to one laptop per child, the following simple invitation should also be given to each participating OLPC student: "In a series of drawings, paintings, photographs, and/or short digital movies, tell the story of the ways your new laptop changes your life, your family, and your community during the first year that you own your laptop." These visual narratives would have to be accompanied by written or oral narratives in the voice or hand of the student, interpreting the set of images that are submitted. Awards for the most evocative stories—communicating the most information—might also be offered as an incentive to respond to this call for open source feedback on the long-term impact of OLPC. Awards could range from cash economic incentives or funding for the future education of that child.

Dr. Negroponte was courteous enough to respond, but as I predicted, nothing much came directly from the conversation. I was an unknown variable. I did however want to put the ideas on paper in order to start a train of thought. Since this correspondence, I have imagined the following: given the likelihood that many of these laptops will be used outside of typical schooling contexts, what if each learner also possessed a personal "black box" of some sort—a kind of digital media storage device and personal document scanner used to record and archive the narrative arc of the self-initiated innovations undertaken by that learner in finding his or her own uses for their laptop? The data-gathering technology already exists and can be utilized in this or any similar initiative to increase global access to technology.

With these precedents in mind now that I am a few years removed from this initial correspondence, I propose that new corporate or foundation sponsorship be solicited to fund what might be called a "Black Box Narrative and Curriculum-Making Challenge," highlighting the utility of their own educational funding programs as well as OLPC'S information technology (or some equivalent), and also providing for an embedded source of metrics tracking the effectiveness of their initiatives. Host nations for the "Black Box Narrative and Curriculum-Making Challenge" might also be convinced that this would be a showcase of the intellectual and creative ingenuity of their youngsters and a promotional magnet for further investment into their educational infrastructure by outside donors. How much different the contents of each "black box," than the glyphs of the Rosetta Stone or the pyramids? The contents of each "black box" can inform us of aspects of the human story we would never have known had the data gone unrecorded. There is no reason for these moments to be lost in time, "like tears in the rain."[9] If nothing else, the "black box" contents might crowd-source new ways to adaptively mimic once-invisible intercultural learning strategies for the common good.

SWARM INTELLIGENCE PROPOSAL #2—THE HUMAN RIGHTS INITIATIVE

What if we were to understand the arts as a basic human right— namely, the right to represent and reinterpret personal and social significance in a way that generates a positive self-image and cultural valuation? Art-making is universally practiced in some form by every nation, every people group, and every civilization. For the arts to be practiced so ubiquitously, they must be absolutely and innately necessary.

Rendering meaning artistically from life and thereby leaving behind the residuals of one's existence can be argued as a basic human right because all people, all cultures, and all civilizations at one point or another must assert to others that they mattered, made a difference, or were simply here. To assert anything less is to accept invisibility and meaninglessness. Perhaps the most crucial of all human rights is then the right to signify self, to signify experience, affinities, aspirations, beliefs, and ideas. Without the liberty to mark oneself as a person who matters—to model one's personal and social experience to others without censorship, and to make special one's place in the world without retribution, prohibition, or diminishment—human agency is curtailed. Agency is conceived here not as the "freedom to do whatever the subject wills but rather freedom to constitute oneself in an unexpected manner—to decode and recode one's identity."[10]

The practice of interpreting and reinterpreting life meaning, or decoding and recoding the meaning of one's identity, is the art of self-determination. It would be simplistic to assume that the act of self-determination is self-serving. Self-determination is actually an agency for the growth of the human superorganism. Olivia Gude points out the role of self-determination in the development of democracy and vigorous community exchange: "It is useful to remember that as educators we create citizens of a democratic society, not so much by filling students with ideas or facts about democracy, as by creating the conditions through which youth experience the pleasures, anxieties, and responsibilities of democratic life."[11]

There are countless historical incidents where the outcomes of arts practice went beyond demanding the protection of human rights and being about something needed, and instead *became* the very thing that was needed. The Harlem Renaissance and the Black Arts movements were actually human rights movements. Picasso's Cubist monochromatic painting of *Guernica* innovated a new form for relating the trauma of war atrocities. The populism and protest in Woody Guthrie's "This Land Is Your Land," like the defiant pride in James Brown's "Say It Loud—I'm Black and I'm Proud," was musically broadcast to inform U.S. citizens of beliefs rarely given public expression. Likewise, the documentary photographs of Lewis Wickes Hine were activist texts and catalysts for the transformation of workplace policies that had allowed the use and abuse of child labor in industry.

Each of these works of art was a prompt for greater self-determination and a needed contribution to democratic life, whether embodying the triumph over trauma, enriching the civic imagination, or contributing to the dismantling oppressive cultural legacies. To see the arts as the right to reinterpret social values and as a catalyst for personal, interpersonal, and social exchange and development, one must first see the arts as an "adaptive, dynamic, goal-seeking, self-preserving, and sometimes evolutionary" *system* for perpetuating the human species.[12] With this understanding, the arts are much more than just a generator of activist manifestos, or a universal language for self-expression, or a means of crafting meaningful objects with technical precision. Each time an artistic act distills meaning from experience, it also enlivens the pulse of the human superorganism.

In 1776, Richard Price wrote of "that principle of spontaneity or self-determination which constitutes us agents or which gives us a command over our actions, rendering them properly ours, and not effects of the operation of any foreign cause" or external oppressor.[13] In this light, access to the arts practices are also an extension of this very same inalienable right—a self-determining means through which to aggregate, accommodate, and assimilate ways of thinking not our own and likewise disseminate our own valued meanings and resources to others. Arts practice sustains the human superorganism and our capacity to convey the significance of the truths we hold self-evident to the next generation.

Without the right to represent self as one sees fit, individuals become invisible. Through the arts, our social constructs, cultures, and civilizations bond and cohere on high moral ground, namely, the agreement to mutually benefit one another such that enduring social structures might be erected. Stuart Hall shares a useful insight regarding human identity construction and site selections for one's representation in society:

> [W]e...occupy our identities very retrospectively: having produced them, we then know who we are. We say, "Oh, that's where I am in relation to this argument and for these reasons." So, it's exactly the reverse of what I think is the common sense way of understanding it, which is that we already know our "self" and then put it out there. Rather, having put it into play...we then discover what we are. I think that only then do we make an investment in it, saying, "Yes, I like that position, I am that sort of person, I'm willing to occupy that position."[14]

Hall is suggesting here that the selection of sites upon which to build self-image and to self-determine identity is a constant process. Along a spectrum from our youngest learners to adult learners, the site selection process in the construction of a vital self-image often presents itself in the form of play and risk-taking. We first construct identity haphazardly—as if we were trying on costumes—in order to differentiate ourselves, locate our peer groups, and find like-minded communities. The early shape of identity can easily shift, and construction sites are typically discarded as easily as they are collected, as if we were playing dress-up games in kindergarten.

The sites of self-image in society are also *contested*, primarily by those who have presumed the power throughout history to control the development and the destinies of young learners, minority people groups, or colonized nations, but sometimes also by those who simply struggle with self-image. A 2011 documentary titled *Precious Knowledge* is an example of contested self-image, telling the story of Arizona legislators who are attempting to purge all ethnic studies from school curricula.[15] A 2012 documentary titled *Dark Girls* highlights the crabs-in-a-barrel phenomenon of self-image being wounded by those who share a wounded self-image.[16]

With these precedents in mind, I propose that instead of the popular *Scholastic Awards* for individual achievement in the creative arts, "Self-Image Awards" might be popularized in places of learning across the nation from the philosophical standpoint of empowering those who do not necessarily see themselves as artists in portraying their own identities, strengths, and points of view in the world. Awards could be given for the creative products of university-community collaborative workshops held regularly in Saturday and summer programs. These "Self-Image Workshops" would be based on an expanded understanding that the purpose of art education goes far beyond facilitating self-expression.

The aim of these "Self-Image Workshops" would be to open up clearings for each student to practice a self-refinement of the image they see reflected of themselves in the world. The work produced would allow for an eclectic assembly of material choices and components for portraiture, self-portraiture, self-image, and the transformation of the face of one's community. Teachers, students, and classmates would have the opportunity to confer and collaborate in varying degrees on the content of each canvas, assemblage, or installation produced, as well as the mediums and methods selected (background imagery, materials, embedded literature quotes, etc.).

In any "Self-Image Workshop," arts practice and arts education would converge. Arts explorations might be organized in themes such as:

- "Self-Image" collaborations—Who am I? Where do I come from?
- "Vision" collaborations—Whom do I desire to be? How should others see me?
- "Home" collaborations—Where do I call home? What is our common ground with those who share our borders?
- "Opinion" collaborations—What do I stand for? What do I stand against?
- "Agency" collaborations—What do I do best? What community do I stand with?
- "Freedom" collaborations—Let me cast off all that so easily hinders!
- "Responsibility" collaborations—What cause compels me? Who am I responsible for?
- "Legacy" collaborations—What have I inherited? What must we pass on?

The purpose of these "Self-Image" projects, workshops and awards would be to open up pathways for adaptive mimicking that ultimately work to feed and support the greater human superorganism. We can do better.

SWARM INTELLIGENCE PROPOSAL #3—THE ARTS ENTREPRENEURSHIP INITIATIVE

What if the arts were valued as a force for economic development, not merely as an investment vehicle for the rich or a means for subsistence income through the sale of souvenirs to tourists? In the *Oscar*-nominated 2010 film *Waste Land*, Brazilian-born artist Vik Muniz travels to Jardim Gramacho—at the time the world's largest landfill site—located on the outskirts of Rio de Janeiro.

Living back in Brazil for well over a year, Muniz worked together on art projects with several *catadores*—the term for the people who pick day and night through mountains of trash, gathering recyclable materials for a meager living.

Muniz collaborated on large-scale portraits, made out of materials plucked and sorted from the landfill and then mapped atop giant photographic projections of these "pickers" on a warehouse floor, posed either as themselves or as characters from the world of art—a world far outside their own. Muniz then photographed the massive portraits assembled from what was once other people's garbage using a bird's eye mounted camera. The final project photos were then auctioned so that sales proceeds could be given back to the workers to enrich the possibilities in their lives. Auctioned photos fetched amounts as high as $64,000 and these royalties helped lift the participating *catadores* out of the poverty and ugliness of Jardim Gramacho, as well as to found "a library, medical clinic, day care center, and a skills training center" intended to help other *catadores* in transitioning to better jobs.[17]

While the taint and odor of garbage relegated the workers to one of the lowest classes in a caste-conscious Brazil, the dignity with which they made their livings and contributed to the creative selection and positioning of garbage throughout their portraits makes an important point. These *catadores* were invited to participate in changing their own lives; in a landscape of waste, they did not squander their opportunity to envision themselves in a whole new frame, discovering and asserting their right to reinterpret self-image. The driving principle behind Muniz's brief intervention into the lives of the *catadores* was not profit; it was altruism.

Altruism is recognized as "a cultural behavior, well beyond instinctive behavior, and even beyond adaptive social behaviors with respect to evolutionary processes."[18] Likewise, the arts and design practices are clearly prominent in the survival of all cultures. What if we reevaluated these aesthetic practices so that they figured centrally as a critical operational mode in the creation of even our economic landscapes? If it is in our biobehavioral DNA to remake our world through art and design, then our art and design outcomes should naturally reflect "the cultural process by which societies have created their living environments."[19] And that includes our economic environments.

In a January 2012 *Inc.com* article by Nicole Carter, entrepreneur Howard Leonhardt was interviewed about his effort to launch a new kind of stock exchange that caters toward the initial financing of start-ups and other small business enterprises.[20] A stock is a share held in a particular company, venture, or industry that is purchased based on the overall value assessed by a shareholder and the portion of that value they are willing to underwrite as an investment. Frustrated at the amount of money entrepreneurs have to spend raising money and at the obstacle course of regulations and fees that often delays fundraising, Leonhardt has begun building the California Stock Exchange with the aim of attracting local investors to raise start-up capital, whether the need is $20,000 or $2 million.

Leonhardt's stock exchange is a form of *crowdfunding*, defined as "the collective effort of individuals who network and pool their money, usually via the Internet, to support efforts initiated by other people or organizations," a concept that has also become popular on digital platforms such as Kickstarter, Indiegogo, RocketHub, and Rock The Post.[21] Crowdfunding is a form of swarm intelligence based on the ideas of microfinancing and crowdsourcing; it is a method for raising money through relatively small contributions from a large swarm of individuals who discover a strong affinity for the story behind your idea. A close relative of the crowdsourcing concept is the microfinancing social bank founded by Bangladeshi economist and 2006 Nobel Peace Prize winner Muhammad Yunus to combat global poverty. The Grameen Bank makes small loans without requiring collateral based on the premise that the poor have valuable skills that are underutilized, and the promise of local peer pressure in ensuring that the loan is eventually repaid. This "microcredit" initiative is described as follows: "In simple terms, a Grameen social business a non-loss, non-dividend company dedicated entirely to achieve a social goal. In social business, the investor gets his/her investment money back over time, but never receives dividend beyond that amount. The Grameen Bank is a prime example of social business, with poor people being its shareholders!"[22]

With these precedents in mind, I propose the crowdsourcing of a global stock exchange solely for socially responsible arts and design outcomes. This Arts Entrepreneurship Exchange, as it might be called, would invite individual investors, community organizations, and municipal, state, and federal governments alike to purchase arts and design investment bonds financing the creative outcomes deemed the most beneficial to local and national swarms of social interaction.

This arts and design stock exchange holds the potential to become a venue for reinvesting in the development of culture-building practices as a vital natural resource, replenishing the many human and environmental resources that have been nearly exhausted or entirely plundered over centuries of empire-building for profit. The purpose of this exchange won't be to corner the art market or generate dividend payouts to stakeholders, but rather to generate new kinds of markets generating altruistic distributions to valued causes (like the Newman's Own food company which directs 100 percent of its profits after taxes to selected educational and charitable organizations).

If arts and design outcomes came to be used as tradable stock market options, they would also become a form of currency for investing in the development of the human superorganism. But there are other possibilities for turning creativity unto currency. What if there were special state lotteries where, to win something you had to make something? I suggest that participation in any one of the 50 "Creative Currency" state lotteries that might be established should require the entry "fee" of both a dollar and a small postcard sized piece of art or design. The proceeds from the pool of lottery funds can be split between the lottery winner and support for the start-up of a pre-designated socially responsible organization. One of the creative works submitted to enter the lottery might be selected by a jury to be used by the start-up organization as part of an inaugural logo, with royalties being paid to the artist or designer for an agreed period of time.

Another form of creative currency might be the institution of "Arts and Design Innovation Fairs" and "Swarm Intelligence Creative Showcases," the same way we hold science fairs and robotics competitions but with an emphasis on celebrating and rewarding a team for its artistic collaboration and civic imagination. In these fairs and showcases, held in schools and on college campuses throughout the nation, the visual arts and design, music, dance, and theatrical performance might regularly be put to work addressing specific local and global needs or problems.

In summary, behave like you're part of a superorganism—*imagine beyond yourself*. Typically, we must be enticed to imagine beyond ourselves. The more common the sense of the value of these enticements, the more traffic there will be in advantageous directions. In the following chapter, I will explore the most simple and most powerful enticements of all to the human mind, the stories we live by.

CHAPTER SIX

STORIES

NARRATIVES OF SWARM INTELLIGENCE TO LIVE BY

The recent Harry Potter readership phenomenon was incredible to behold. This serial narrative produced seven wildly popular and widely read books by author J. K. Rowling, which were published between 1997 and 2007 to both critical acclaim and commercial success. This series of stories has gone on to spawn movies, websites, e-books, and various other highly anticipated merchandise. This is truly astounding for a work of children's literature, moreover one that stands as an exemplar of the fantasy genre that is uniquely centered around the theme of death. Despite its heavy subject matter, the narrative arc of Harry Potter's struggle to overcome the deadly forces set against him since he was an infant were clearly enthralling to each avid reader of Rowling's books. Harry's story was transporting readers somewhere each wanted to go—toward a resolution they could identify with.

In this chapter I consider and present the kinds of narratives that generate the satisfaction of immersive possibilities, beckoning others to come along for the ride with tantalizing implications of *what-if* questions such as "What if this happened to me?," or "What would I do if I were in Harry's shoes?," or "What if had my own magic wand?," or "Would I act that bravely if I were in the same situation?" These are incomplete narratives. Emergent narratives. Narratives that bubble and percolate into multiple trajectories, generating new stories in their wake. The cliffhanger. The page-turner. The trail marker. In their devotion to J. K. Rowling's books, her characters, and the stories they unfold, the vast community of Harry Potter readers and aficionados—with their costume homages and quidditch sporting competitions and imagined alternative wizarding realities—are simply behaving in concert as a unique creative swarm. While Rowling's influence is indisputable, the list of stories and storytellers that have influenced her writing, both historical and contemporary, is just as immense. In a 2005 BBC radio interview, Rowling reveals:

> I've taken horrible liberties with folklore and mythology, but I'm quite unashamed about that, because British folklore and British mythology is a totally bastard mythology. You know, we've been invaded by people, we've appropriated their gods, we've taken their mythical creatures, and we've soldered them all together to make, what I would say, is one of the richest folklores in the world, because it's so varied. So I feel no compunction about borrowing from that freely, but adding a few things of my own.[1]

The list of stories and storytellers Rowling has reinterpreted includes *The Iliad*, the Bible, Aeschylus, Geoffrey Chaucer,

Shakespeare, Jane Austen, E. Nesbit, children's fantasy writer Kenneth Grahame, Christian essayist and mystery writer Dorothy L. Sayers, and C. S. Lewis, the author of *The Chronicles of Narnia*, amongst many others.[2] This incredible swarm of thinkers and their successful effort to convey human values, memory and meaning through their literature represents the ongoing power of story to shape the continuum of creative social intelligence.

STORIES THAT ENTICE US TO THINK DIFFERENTLY

In nature, one of the keys to marshaling a multitude of decentralized advantageous actions into a single cumulative advantage to the entire swarm is in each agent's release of "virtual pheromones" which, like the excreted or secreted attractors in ant colonies, act as enticements triggering a likewise advantageous social response in the members of their community. But since chemicals or computer algorithms are not a primary attractor for human beings, what are the most prominent enticements in our creative swarms?

The creation of beauty is an enticement—whether its format is written, performed, sung, danced, or given visual form. So is the creation of authentic, familiar, or resonant expressions of meaning—these never fail to entice. For others, the most enticing thing imaginable is hearing someone say the words you knew needed to be said in an urgent, incisive, and meaningful critique of the circumstances at hand. In other words, enticements vary. They are the approaches to tasks or solutions to problems that make the most sense to an individual or the most common sense in that particular learning community or social group. Where these enticements are shared and passed along, others will follow. What are the enticements of the human swarm? Very simply, the stories we live by.

Plato made the observation that "stories form the natural food of the young."[3] But upon further observation, stories feed our understandings throughout the entirety of our lives. A story, once interpreted, becomes food for thought; the more stories interpreted, the greater and healthier the scope of an individual's development. The more diverse cultural and personal stories interpreted throughout the core of a civilization, the greater and healthier the scope of that civilization's collective creativity. Our need for newly imagined stories cannot be overstated, a need so great there is considerable danger in using adult standards and conventions as tethers, reeling in children too early from the narrative possibilities they navigate on immaturity's sea.[4] It has been argued: "Our capacity to tell a story…is not something that we wish to lose. It is more than just a feature of our childhood because it plays a vital role in adult consciousness and is most active when we begin to learn something new. To put it as simply and straightforwardly as possible, we begin to learn something new with a story in mind."[5]

When I was in graduate school, in response to a class assignment one of my peers documented a small bit of primary research on the differing meanings of "art" that people hold in mind. His interview subject recalled a true story of discovery that went on to shape his identity as an artist:

When I was thirteen I took a trip to Italy with my family and we saw Michelangelo's "Moses." Which made me shake. It was the first time I saw something that struck me. I think my heart stopped. Since then I have made trips to see that sculpture. When I was eighteen I returned to San Pietro in Vincoli (St. Peter in Chains) to see the sculpture. I spent a whole day looking at it. Sometimes the Church was overrun with tour bus groups and other times I was all alone. That first experience when I was thirteen blew me away. I later returned when I was in my twenties, and also when Mary and I took our honeymoon; we went to Italy and we returned together. I specifically wanted to show her that piece. [Michelangelo's] "David" may be the perfect sculpture but my emotions that are connected to the Moses sculpture proved to be a pivotal experience. It was to feel my metabolism change.

This particular interview subject went on to study and apprentice as a sculptor and object-maker. He became changed in an encounter with a visual story about the biblical character of Moses carved from a block of marble centuries ago. What advantages do stories this powerful yield? Stories cause minds that initially think and do nothing alike to suddenly chase ahead together toward the front of the pack. Stories provoke minds that are boxed into uncomfortable or imposed constraints and circumstances to separate themselves from the hindering crowd. Stories bring insular, entrenched thinking into an open-throttle and interactive alignment with other minds set free to roam. Stories sweep the chaos of diverse elements that comprise the larger human story into common narratives, myths, and fables helping us to arrive together at the next phase in our social evolution with the same shared hopes and possibilities in mind.

What kinds of stories make for the most powerful enticements? Some stories are *hidden narratives*, the start of a swarm of interaction that asks, *What stories are unseen?* These are the stories that provoke curiosity, wonder, and sometimes bewilderment at all that had been previously overlooked. Some stories are *vicarious narratives*, the start of a swarm of interaction that asks, *What other stories might function in place of my own experience?* These are the stories that wake us up to what we could not have otherwise known or believed if we had not escaped our own skins for a time to surround and absorb the thoughts of another individual. Yet other stories are *alternative narratives*, the start of a swarm of interaction that asks, *What stories have now become possible through this storytelling? What stories are exploded?* These are the stories that move us all forward from current mission into newfound vision and invention.

There have always been stories of prodigies among us. Where does this prodigiousness come from? From whence does a prodigy emerge? Here is a fact. No prodigy is formed in a vacuum. A recent article in the *Smithsonian* magazine tells the story of young Jack Andraka who, at fifteen years old, is considered a prodigy because of his invention of a new method to detect lethal pancreatic cancer. And yet as his mentor—Anirban Maitra, a Johns Hopkins Hospital pathologist and pancreatic cancer researcher—reflects on how the invention came to the boy's mind, he inadvertently reveals the power of multiple, interacting stories to rewire and rewrite individual thinking.

The Science paper he was covertly reading at his desk was about applications for nanotubes. With half an ear, Andraka listened to his biology teacher lecture on antibodies, which bind to particular proteins in the blood. Suddenly, the two ideas collided in his mind. What if he could lace a nanotube network with mesothelin-specific antibodies, then introduce a drop of a pancreatic cancer patient's blood? The antibodies would bind to the mesothelin and enlarge. These beefed-up molecules would spread the nanotubes farther apart, changing the electrical properties of the network: The more mesothelin present, the more antibodies would bind and grow big, and the weaker the electrical signal would become. Other scientists had recently designed similar tests for breast and prostate cancers, but nobody had addressed pancreatic cancer. "It's called connecting the dots," Maitra says.[6]

Much more than a connection of dots, what happened in Jack Andraka's head was a collision of stories—and in that collision, two unrelated sets of ideas from other like-minded thinkers about nanotubes and antibodies were also thrown together, one mediating the other. Andraka suddenly noticed the emergent story about a way to detect pancreatic cancer that had not yet been made visible to others. It's like Michelangelo's famous ability to fully envision the completed but as-yet-uncarved winged archangel within the solid block of marble standing before him. Andraka's invention was right there in the swirl of blending stories before him, in the stir of ideas from a swarm of prior thinkers—it doesn't matter whether those ideas were spoken into his ear by his teacher or written on a page. The invention was there all along and he was simply the first not to overlook it. We too often make the mistake of focusing on the prodigy and not on the swarm of thinkers and doers that foster prodigious thinking.

HOW THE INDIVIDUAL BRAIN CONVERTS STORIES INTO SWARM INTELLIGENCE

The rules of the creative swarm are simple: follow the trail of the fish in front, if there is one ahead of you, and keep pace with the fish beside you. All of the traits and characteristics of human creativity also follow from these rules. The larger the network of agents within any given swarm, the more exponential are the possible configurations of ideas and shared actions that might ultimately emerge from it as each individual navigates pathways that make life and growth even more viable. These principles are so simple in fact, it is a lot easier than we think to allow our classrooms and schools to behave as self-organizing social networks where the teachers understand themselves as participating agents, rather than viewing themselves as primarily responsible for regimenting the behavior of all the other younger agents. In truth, students already know everything they need to know about how to follow the rules and where those rules are located. Our social rules are *always* hidden in plain sight and codified within the stories we make up, retell, and pass along to one another. Bedtime stories and children's picture books, told and retold, are more than recreation. They are guidebooks. But how do stories first impress themselves upon our imagination? How then do they rise to the surface of consciousness and become a part of our everyday lexicon?

A recent *TIME* magazine article on brain physiology points out that the human brain, like the other organs of a living human body, is never fully shut down—it is continually processing the daily inflow of information, even its dreams.[7] The processing of social information from the local swarm is mediated in the shape of stories. There is a good reason for this. Consider for a moment the catalytic converter in an automobile. Its purpose in a car's engine is to convert the more poisonous byproducts from the engine's exhaust—hydrocarbons, carbon monoxide, and nitrogen oxides—into harmless compounds. Similarly, the impediments to the human superorganism are those products of common social interaction that are poisonous to every individual: chaos, conflict, and complacency. The story-making function of the individual's brain is the catalytic converter for human social relations. Here is how.

The chaos of multiple, diverse members of one's local swarm as they think and act and independently influence is first introduced to the brain as disassociated gibberish, impeding swarm intelligence. But the brain rejects chaos as dangerous because it offers no cues for individual behavior in response. Without an intelligible and guiding narrative to read and to act upon, the individual is paralyzed regarding which movements they are to mimic and adapt. Hence, one of the keys to the brain's processing is to slow down the gibberish that impedes individual decision-making processes within a human swarm. Converting the chaos of behaviors typically on display within one's social networks into creative and beneficial action requires the following brain-based individual responses to social experience, turning stimulus into story:

1. *Observation*, of the surrounding stories colliding throughout the swarm, embodying some as stories to live by.

2. *Making Metaphor*, the meditative act of drawing reference points and salient features from newly encountered stories into the reservoir of memory where our first stories are secured—and then playing with possibilities for re-drawing the maps of initial meaning.

3. *Idle Time* or *Idyll Time,* powering down, spending time at rest from the acquisition of new information from outside stimuli so as to focus on the internal resolution of meaningful stories— whether by diverted focus given toward daydreaming, or within the default cognitive awareness that produces nightdreams while in the state of sleep.

4. *Active Innovation*, powering back up, allowing the unconsidered story to emerge from the mash-up of observations, reference points, and free mental space to adapt new meaning.

The conflict over what information is worth processing into reference points for new story possibilities is intense, also impeding swarm intelligence. In the film *The Matrix*, there is a savvy insight revealed by the story's writers, the Wachowski brothers. What is the Matrix? The Matrix is the mainframe wherein all social life is enacted, and where all behaviors are manifested. It is a kaleidoscope of narrative cross-currents. All social behavior—everything that happens "out there" is reducible to a scroll of moving patterns that, once connected into the brain, are interpreted and navigated—ultimately, they can even be rewritten "in here." Likewise, the social behavior of others in our own social worlds— the creative input and output of all surrounding swarms—must be interfaced and converted into small, utilitarian narratives and cues for personal behavior. In other words, the true gifting of each individual thinker is in our facility as catalytic converters of the chaos and confusion of everyday life, rendered harmless as stories to live by.

A CLOSER LOOK AT OBSERVATION

The power of story in shaping swarm intelligence begins with the observation of stories from the surrounding swarm. When I was young, I was an architect of sorts; I built stories in my head based on the things I saw. I was a student at P.S. 52 in middle-class Sheepshead Bay in Brooklyn, bussed there from my home a world away in a distant and largely lower-income neighborhood called Crown Heights. The bus ride to school each morning was as alienating as it was exhilarating.

At the close of my first grade school year, my teacher, Mrs. Erenrich, gave me a gift that plugged me directly into the swarm—she gave me books. She let me select them, from *Curious George* to *Ants and Bees*. The latter book on the hidden life of insects was particularly fascinating to me with its cross-sectional visual renderings of the underground chambers in an ant colony and those hidden inside a beehive. I was asthmatic as a child and it inhibited all typical boyhood exertions—running in circles, around baseball diamonds, up and down courts, after others—all restricted. In place of running, what I learned to do exceptionally well was to quietly watch others at play, at work, or just passing the time. Back at home after school, I was often found stooped over the small but numerous anthills in my front yard as a motionless observer. But while I have long maintained a practice as a conscious observer of the world around me, the brain of *every* individual is wired to perceive the world as a stimulus for general cognitive functioning, growth, and development—whether that individual is conscious of it or not.

In *The Literary Mind*, Mark Turner makes the claim that the human mind in its everyday functioning is essentially literary in its activity. He does so, firstly, in suggesting that the narrative imagination and our ability to generate and interpret meaningful stories is the basic instrument of everyday thought, upon which all other rational capacities depend, especially our planning, predictive, and explanatory aptitudes as we try to make sense of life within the surrounding swarm. Secondly, Turner asserts that the mind exercises the capacity first to meditate on stories and then to tell new stories, projecting one story upon another as we contemplate them in mind and relate to one another. Drawing from the original Greek definition of the word *parable* as "the tossing or projecting of one thing alongside another," the projection of story—or parable—is presented by Turner as one of our most important mental processes in the construction of meaning, indispensable to swarm intelligence by allowing us to find the overlaps between multiple and diverse strains of knowledge.[8]

Turner argues that the projection of story is fundamental to the construction of meaning. But if so, the projection of story is also the beginning of the process that tosses out stories as enticements to other members of the human swarm. Turner carries his examination of the phenomenon of parable back to early childhood thinking and the pre-language state of mind. According to Turner's theory, rudimentary stories must exist in mind before the development of oral and literary language skills, or else the ability to make ongoing sense of life experience is doomed at the outset. Turner argues that the basic narrative tool during the pre-language state is what he terms a "spatial story."

Prior to language development, these are stories of small events experienced in the crib, on the mat, in the sandbox, in the tub—in those spaces first familiar to children as they arrive at an understanding of the larger space they must initially occupy, and then navigate, in the world. These spatial stories are concrete and physical encounters with objects and bodies in space, understood through the five senses—episodes that take place within a containment, or overflowing containment; locomotive episodes, or episodes inert of locomotion; episodes that initiate an action, yield to an action, resist an action, or result in an action. These small stories of events in childhood's limited spatial boundaries are fundamental encounters with the world we live in. We first come to know these stories through repeated touching, tasting, hearing, smelling, and viewings. The raw emotions triggered by those encounters entrench them in mind forever thereafter.

Spatial stories are basic stories, the stories we've known longest, the stories we know best: Daddy picks me up; Mommy puts me in the water; the wind blows across my face; the rain falls on my tongue; Mommy pours the milk into the glass; I balance my toy soldier on top of the blocks; that other little boy throws the rock—kerplunk!—into the pond; the bird goes up into the air; the fish swims around in the tank; the ants march in and out of the anthill; the train goes through the tunnel; the leaf is carried away by the stream; the rubber ball bounces until it bounces no more; that sound makes me cry.

We will learn these stories with numbing repetition if necessary, yet as we learn them we are utterly absorbed. Furthermore, we discover they are endlessly connective, possessing a component quality to enable our sense of more complex story episodes in life and possibilities for changing the script. Hence, our first and most fundamental story understandings afford the necessary models to aid the more complex understanding that, for instance, "[t]o walk in the rain, we must go *outside* of our *house-container* so we will not be *under* a roof that *stops* the rain from *falling down onto* us, and we must *move* along a *path out of* doors.[9] In fact, our first notions of what is impossible begins with these stories—this is why simple magic tricks and illusions are so enthralling as we are forced to make sense of small episodes that collide with our most fundamental understandings of how the world works and is not supposed to work.

Spatial stories thus render themselves foundational to all language learning to follow—before language, we are already in firm possession of tools that we have used successfully in arriving at a particularly human experience of how the world works, its boundaries, and how we affect the world. Our foundational understandings of the common spatial experiences we all share give us something universally sensible to talk about—we would talk and think differently if we all flew to and fro like birds or possessed gills and could breathe underwater or lived solely in tree canopies. Even if the oral staccato of our native language is unintelligible to one another, we all understand that *up* feels fundamentally different than *down* and that *here* is separate from *there*. For this reason, our personal spatial stories become what cognitive scientist and philosopher Mark Johnson has described as "image schemata," the maps we use for picturing the world in mind and conveying meaningful stories about it both verbally and visually.

> If we are to experience our world as a connected and unified place that we can make sense of, then there must be repeatable pattern and structure in our experiences. Image schemata *are* those *recurring structures of, or in, our perceptual interactions, bodily experiences, and cognitive operations.* These schematic structures have a relatively small number of parts or components that stand in very definite relations to one another. So whenever a single schema is instantiated in a number of different experiences or images, these same parts and relations recur.[10]

In other words, the stories we live by seek out ways to connect with one another. A rudimentary lexicon of life's little everyday episodes prepares our pattern recognition abilities to follow their threads of meaning through subsequent episodes while rendering us perceptive of the larger compounding stories that make us human together. Feminist scholar Bronwyn Davies writes about the narratives of living and notes that as children "we learn the patterns and meanings of our language as embodied patterns and meanings."[11] But in order to see the larger map of stories that make us who we are and the emergent stories pushing up from beneath the surface like new land formations as stories interact, we must first meditate on how our initial understandings fit together with the new information about the world that we receive daily.

WHERE METAPHORS ARE MADE

Our initial sense of the world and our place in it just isn't good enough. Each day, we continue to encounter new stimuli and new stories to consider living by, altering the landscapes of our living like the tectonic plates of the Earth's crust scraping against each other on a sea of magma. We must continue therefore to *make* sense. What is the brain's process for re-drawing the maps of initial meaning and developing the architecture for new understandings? The answer is in the brain's facility for making new meaning through metaphor.

In everyday thought, as in all forms of education, the mind seeks to align and compare. Cognition is a perpetual filtering process—the mind compares and then retains or jettisons information as meaningful or meaningless when juxtaposed with what is already known. The mind creates archetypes from its first known events, first possessed objects, and first attempts to navigate through space, labeling them familiar. But the mind might just as well rename the unfamiliar as familiar, or banish the unfamiliar as unknowable. The things that are most familiar become the stories we tell over and over again. The language of those stories is constituted of the metaphors we make of lived experience: "We cannot speak without speaking metaphorically—as our spoken languages are constructed from symbolic building materials that are metaphorical in nature. Words are only symbols for their meanings. One symbol, sign, word, object, or idea *represents* another.... Our symbolic minds work by implicitly relating different things and processes. Through metaphors, we may relate something we know to something we don't."[12]

The mind aligns and compares the multiple sources of lived experience—experience that has already been embodied, and new experiential encounters. Try this experiment. Waggle a fingertip directly in front of one of your eyes, almost brushing the eyelashes, while the other eye is held shut. Next, keep waggling your finger, but close the eye you had originally been waggling the finger in front of while at the same time opening the eye without a finger in front of it. Finally, keep waggling your finger and open both eyes at the same time. Remember, your finger should have been in motion throughout this experiment. Now, reflect. One eye was telling the story of a waggling object—one too close for comfort, dangerously eclipsing one's vision. This was a partial understanding. At the same time, the other eye told a story of no impediment to sight whatsoever, also a partial understanding. Yet with both eyes open, the two sources of information *blended* in cognition to create the more complete understanding that there was just a finger waggling in front of one's left or right eye, but not the other.

While this is a simple spatial story, the cognitive ability to blend information pathways and meld concepts into a fuller understanding remains intact even as the concepts multiply in number, or the information they supply increases in complexity. What is the formula for these blendings, these acts of reinterpretation? In *The Literary Mind*, Mark Turner draws upon George Lakoff's definition of metaphor as consisting of these elements:

- a source domain,
- a target domain, and
- a source to target mapping.[13]

Metaphors are formed in mind through juxtaposition. The superimposition of a source concept, or knowledge domain, atop a target perception ultimately creates what Turner defines as a *blended space*, re-mapping both the current sense and future meaning that may be derived from both the source and the target of the metaphor. I offer the following example. The first home my wife and I ever owned was in Plainfield, New Jersey, and since I was on the faculty of Columbia University's new elementary school in Manhattan, I had to commute every day to New York City. One January morning in 2005, I was standing inside the station house of the "Fanwood" New Jersey Transit station on the Raritan line. It was bright and overcast, one day after the remnants of a snowstorm originating from the Midwest had whipped through Union County in the form of a cold, heavy rain.

While I was standing inside the station house with the train soon to arrive, the following incident occurred. I became vaguely aware of a short, wide-bodied woman, not more than five feet, five inches tall, standing almost directly in my line of sight, about twelve feet in front of me, outdoors on the platform beyond the pane of glass. She was wearing a full-length black leather overcoat that spread down past her hips to her calves, black suit pants, black flats, and two black leather carrying bags slung over each of her shoulders, one bag slightly smaller than the other. From where I stood, her face was not at all visible, just a wedge-shaped shock of hazel-colored hair with lots of damaged ends. The woman, on her way to work in New York just like me, was waiting outside in the cold at the platform's edge, a little more eager to board the train than I was. Or, perhaps, simply dressed more warmly.

But what sharpened my perception of her was the large stain across the back of her leather overcoat. It was only on my second look that I noticed the stain sweeping down like the slope of a mountain from an apex just beneath the area of her left shoulder blade, running all the way down the silhouette of her left side against the bare gray bushes across the tracks, back across her buttocks, and cutting off abruptly at a baseline at about mid-thigh. Had she just sat down in some putrid liquid on a bench? Was she unaware or unconcerned that she had left her home in a damaged coat? I doubted both possibilities. She was dressed too sharply, with too much self-awareness. That's when I noticed that the stain was moving.

I took a third hard look, and that's when I realized that the movement I perceived appeared to be the twiddling a pair of almost imperceptible thumbs. Upon my next successive look, I was able to make out the set of disembodied hands those thumbs were attached to—and that's when I finally realized that I had been watching a blend of perceptive events. A reflection of a woman twiddling her thumbs and sitting approximately twelve feet behind me on a bench inside the station house was superimposed on the pane of glass directly in my line of sight and across the black overcoat of the woman on the other side of the glazing.

The longer I looked, the more detailed the spatial metaphor became; I could see the play of light on the rolling suede folds of the camel-colored jacket worn by the woman behind me, pressed beneath the subtly shifting weight of her hands in motion. Yet her headless and legless body fragment revealed the depths of its contours and its visual archaeology only where its reflection fell across the black overcoat. The body fragment was an illusory presence, grossly incompatible within the borders of the stout woman outside at the platform's edge who remained motionless and staring intently down the length of track, watching the triangular array of approaching headlights grow larger. These two women—oblivious to one another—were also simultaneously apparent and inextricable from one another, occupying a blended space within my perception.

These spatial and conceptual metaphors of lived experience, or blended spaces, can be seen as emergent domains of knowledge and understanding. Through the brain's metaphorical mechanisms, the source concept of childhood can be mapped over the target form of a ragged teddy bear, imbuing the stuffed animal with a story that tells of home and safety and the warmth of a mother's hugs; a story of stability and manhood can be evinced in the rediscovery of the old toy ray gun Daddy bought for your birthday as it is once again held in hand; watching a group of kids engaged in a whirling, rhyming song can tell a story of lost friendships as it maps over the memory of the last time you played the game. The athletic achievement of an underdog team can be rendered as a metaphor for national pride. Close relatives can be shunned as symbols of a painful childhood event. Whole groups of people can be cast as representatives of savagery, defect, ugliness, or evil.

Turner further argues that source concepts and target perceptions "can be not only *providers* of projections to the blend, but also *receivers* of projections back from the developed blend."[14] These are the blended spaces where metaphors are made, creating new episodes and interpretations of the human story. When we tell the human story, in music, in theater, in an image, in text, we narrate ourselves. As a society generates new metaphors important to its survival, it hoards those as stories. How? These metaphors are artfully spoken and spoken through art. They are memorized and recorded. They are retold and rehearsed. Hence, they are retained not just in individual memory but also in the reservoir of public memory.

DOWN TIME

There are two kinds of down time known to be crucial to everyday mental processing—idle time and idyll time. *Idle time* refers to the state of deep sleep, when all primary mental systems power down and nightdreaming becomes the staging platform for integrating newly received perceptions and newly constructed metaphors into the general cognitive architecture. *Idyll time* refers to a waking state of mental deactivation known as daydreaming that is more important than you ever realized in making sense of the world as we experience it. In fact, it is becoming more apparent that both idle time and idyll time ultimately accomplish the same purpose as scientists continue to uncover "the striking continuity between nightdreaming and daydreaming and the ability of creative people to harness this continuity."[15]

Research shows that when most of us fall asleep, the brain network that involves attention to the outside world (the working memory network consisting primarily of the lateral frontal and parietal cortices) deactivates and our default brain network (medial prefrontal and posterior cingulate cortices) takes over. The discovery of the default brain network is important, as it involves various aspects of our self, such as our self-representations, dreams, imagination, current concerns, autobiographical memory and perspective-taking ability.[16]

During deep rapid eye movement (REM) sleep, when the conscious mind is idle, the story fragments and captured imagery of lived experience are unbound and then mixed and reconnected "the wrong way," allowing what are known as "binding errors" to surreptitiously unfold into "other, untried avenues" of thinking. The conscious awareness works most efficiently when it focuses on one thing at a time; the default unconscious awareness utilizes nightdreaming as a means for making sense of the experiential mess of stimuli from the preceding day by processing loads of recorded information along multiple "parallel pathways."[17] During REM sleep, the brain simultaneously searches old neural networks while constructing new arrays of synaptic connections so that stored information can most easily be recalled again in the form of experiential stories. A key organ of the brain's architecture for making useful sense is called the *hippocampus*.

An example of the importance of the hippocampus is my recollection of the importance of this obscure piece of brain architecture during this writing. I literally woke up one morning with the hippocampus on my mind. I jotted down this physiological term in pencil on the side of an envelope as I hopped out of bed. The hippocampus is a small seahorse-shaped formation deep inside the medial temporal lobe of the brain that appears to be essential for the consolidation of memory. It is considered a part of the cerebral cortex and is a piece of the brain's architecture that I have only written about once with any great focus, over ten years ago. A crucial component in the consolidation of both long-term and short-term memory, the hippocampus tries to provide a complete and coherent picture of life experience even if all the pieces of an event are not there within an individual's recollection, or is not consistent. The hippocampus will even draw upon unrelated experiences or imagined visual memories to construct a coherent view of the world.

That piece of writing on the hippocampus so many years ago was just what I needed to refer to in order to complete this chapter section. But I would never have recalled that writing unless I had fallen asleep on the problem I was wrestling with—a signal of the importance of down time in the mental processing of experiential stories. And poetically, that is the very function of the hippocampus—to comb through all the existing synaptic pathways of the brain, braiding in new information where it makes sense—so that crucial bits of embedded information can be recalled and floated to the surface of awareness attached to the tether lines the brain has woven throughout its experiential memory, its network of essential stories.

It is also important to note that the default processing system that takes place during nightdreaming is an *active* level of awareness, and requires the hippocampus to be fully booted up, so to speak. As already mentioned, this system of memory-making and recollection is booted up during nightdreaming. This is why if one is completely knocked unconscious with the brain's systems thrown offline due to a traumatic head injury, it is often impossible to accurately recall the events of the day leading up to the accident.

The brain's default processing system is also at work during *idyll time*, my term for the tranquil state of mind known as daydreaming—a story-making processing system of the brain with which I am intimately acquainted. My parents bussed all of us Rolling kids to Sheepshead Bay in Brooklyn so we could get a better education than if we stayed in our own neighborhood. As it came to pass, I excelled as a student—yet as one of a handful of African American kids in the school, which was also located in a predominantly White neighborhood, I stood apart from the crowd and was neither made welcome nor given any opportunity to talk about my feelings of displacement. Shortly after elementary school, I skipped seventh grade and began as a student at the High School of Art & Design in midtown Manhattan; I was only twelve years old. Consequently, I began college when I was sixteen years old. Throughout those years, because I was rarely in classes with kids my age or with whom I identified, I always felt invisible. It was difficult to make sense of my loneliness.

To compensate, I learned to daydream. I kept my head so full of images and ideas I didn't have to depend on other people to keep me company. Some kids collected Matchbox cars, or bottle caps or souvenir cards. I did some of that too, but I mainly collected observations and perceptions and daydreamed them into stories, generating associations between diverse and unrelated things that served as cues for my recall. Hence, by the time I had entered high school I was just as interested in art as I was in biology. I was just as interested in architecture as I was in English. I was just as interested in learning the hidden codes and cues required to live from day to day in the generally low-income Crown Heights neighborhood I grew up in, as I was in mastering the cues and codes required to navigate the range of middle-income to rich neighborhoods in Manhattan through which I had to travel on my way to school.

Through my daydreams, I became accustomed to crossing borders. In fact, I started writing poetry in high school and have never stopped. For me, ideas do not fragment into compartments—they bleed into one another freely and I do not attempt to control the admixtures. I learned very early to enjoy being surprised by outcomes and acquisitions of wandering mentally across an open field. In elementary school, I was sometimes chastised for being a daydreamer, but in retrospect what was viewed as a lack of focus was actually a learning strategy. A recent *Huffington Post* article addresses the question of why daydreamers are so creative and caused me to reflect on my habit of keeping a television or radio on in the background when writing, or keeping dozens of folder windows open as I work on my laptop. I need to maintain a level of distraction and mental clutter at my disposal in order to write; it helps me to make a lot of unexpected connections and I've been writing this way for a long time. Popular author and journalist Jonah Lehrer concludes the following: "And this is why distraction is helpful: People unable to focus are more likely to consider information that might seem irrelevant but will later inspire the breakthrough. When we don't know where to look, we need to look everywhere."[18]

It appears that when engaging the brain's default processing systems, the "inability to suppress seemingly unnecessary cognitive activity may actually help creative subjects in associating two ideas represented in different [and initially unrelated] networks" of thinking.[19] Daydreaming has been a successful approach to learning for me as I have navigated across very different social swarms throughout my life experience, a strategy I taught myself as a child and never abandoned. The products of both idle time and idyll time are stored up in the individual imagination only to emerge as story innovations capable of affecting the overall intelligence of the entire swarm.

INNOVATION RISING

At some point, stories first harbored in mind must enter the world. Our experiential stories rise "into the world of objects [and expressed ideas], where men [and women] can look at it."[20] The transmediation of individual experience into the collective consciousness of one's family or classroom or community or nation requires active innovation, wherein new stories are most fully constituted by being physically manifested or conceptually represented. The mediating instruments of an individual's experiential storehouse can involve any natural or manufactured material, object, subject, event, or phenomenon used to describe, explain, or metaphorically interpret some aspect of daily living, relationships, the physical or metaphysical world. Although the active innovation of a new story can be a complex behavior, it is also so simple a child can do it.

Several years ago, I taught as an afterschool teacher at Hunter College Elementary School in New York City. I started off as an instructor in the Hunter "Clubhouse" extended-day program, teaching drawing, painting, poetry, 3-D design, etc., and eventually became the program's director. Each trimester my staff and I attempted to put together a fun and enriching slate of course offerings, and I continued to teach a course or two every so often. I created a class called "*Picture This!*" for the Little Room students, our kindergarteners through first graders. The premise was to offer each child an opportunity to synthesize meaning from his or her experiential store of memories of salient encounters with the world, converting experience into simple word concepts using a methodology of markers and crayons. This was story-making innovation by the children in a rudimentary form, but innovation nonetheless.

For example, in one particular class as we sat around a table, I asked the children the question, "What is big?" I solicited discussion, feedback, points, and counterpoints. One child named Patrick responded, "A dinosaur skull is big." He then recounted a recent museum visit and did a drawing of himself in a large cap standing next to his Dad, the tallest figure in the drawing. This first-grader's concept of "big" was tied to his memory of an experiential, visual/spatial encounter in relation to his own body. In the drawing, Patrick is wearing the large cap, standing next to his Dad (see Figure 1).

Figure 1 Drawing of a "big" head by a Little Room student

At the time of this drawing, I also worked closely with Patrick as an assistant teacher in an inter-grade classroom of first and second graders, so I knew that Patrick's writing skills were quite behind others in his homeroom class. He maintained a passionate distaste for exercising his penmanship and needed extra attention just to maintain focus on his workbook assignments. Nevertheless, Patrick kept a sketchbook and recorded his thoughts daily, primarily in images; in spite of his lack of interest in writing, he had a great capacity to *draw* what was on his mind and being stored up in his imagination. After our after-school class drawing project, by innovating a visual story and placing it on the classroom walls where I hung all finished work for discussion, Patrick had successfully affected his classmates' conception of just how big "big" is.

CINDERELLA STORIES

In society, complacency impedes swarm intelligence, leaving individuals all too accepting of stories as they are—whether they like those stories or not. However, the late author Chinua Achebe once wrote: "*If you don't like someone's story, you write your own.*"[21] For example, the Cinderella fable exists in more than 1,500 variations in cultures and countries around the world. It is a simple story of a life reinterpreted from woundedness to renewal, outsider status to acceptance, and is found among cultures as varied as China, the Eskimo peoples, France, Germany, Zuni Indians, ancient Egypt, and Xhosa Africans.[22] Charles Perrault first published the version of the Cinderella fable we are most familiar with in Paris in 1697. The story remains with us.

In earlier texts of the fable, one of the labels applied by the stepmother and stepsisters to she who would become Cinderella was "Cinderbreech," the equivalent of saying "Cinder-hind parts" or "Cinderbuttocks," the most visible part of her as she crawled about to clean out the chimney debris, and the dirtiest part of her as she was forced to sit among the cinders. Nevertheless, according to the story, she was a hundred times more beautiful than her stepsisters. Why does this story continue to be retold?

I myself have retold the Cinderella story in a recent book, my point of interest being the story of lost identity that culminates in renewed promise, a story that reshapes victimization into a story of agency.[23] My wounds stem from a loss of social identity because of the incalculable disruption of lives and communities captured into slavery from the continent of Africa, later complicated by a purposeful devaluation of African American families in popular culture and society. Demeaning portrayals were colored in with broken crayons representing only the most sweeping generalizations—Bad, Bad Leroy Brown, the brutal black buck; Topsy or Buckwheat, the untamed, unkempt watermelon-eating picaninny; Uncle Tom, the smiling, wide-eyed docile servant; Aunt Jemima, the obese, utterly contented, pitch black maternal figure; Jezebel, the uninhibited whore, denizen of all sexual fantasies; Sambo, the lazy, inarticulate buffoon; Jim Crow or Zip Coon, the vagabond darkie entertainer, or song-and-dance minstrel; Peola, the quadroon, the self-hating mulatto, poisoned with the scourge of Negro blood and the selfishness of white social aspirations; Golliwog, the grotesque and alien rag doll, the antithesis of porcelain-skinned beauty.

In contemporary society, these savage caricatures are further revisited by the stigma of broadcast news formats that predominantly feature the crimes or failings perceived within the Black community as the talking points for explaining the Black experience in America. My retelling of the Cinderella story—of redemption visited upon our lives in unexpected ways and typically when no one sees it coming—also became a means for me to depict African American identity as a continuing and episodic work of art, and the arts we practice as a continuing work of identity.

In the remainder of this chapter, I will present stories from the creative swarm, solicited from others. Stories that change lives. Stories we can live by. It is said that there are only seven basic variations of the human story that we continually recycle, reuse, riff off, and crossbreed: overcoming the monster; rags to riches; the quest; voyage and return; the comedy of errors; the tragedy, aka riches to rags; rebirth. Swarms tend to coalesce around these story variations that move us forward in a quest for rebirth—or at least reinterpretation.

PLAYTIME POLITICS

This first story of swarm intelligence is one common to everyone who attended school as a child. It is sent from a dear friend named Jacqueline Oliver whom I have known for over 20 years and who shares my Caribbean heritage, albeit far less removed in that while I was born in the United States, she was actually born on the island of Jamaica. In a timely exchange, my friend shared the following recollection with me as I was writing this chapter. Oliver—who is studying to enter the field of nursing—has written a *hidden narrative*, telling the unseen inception of altruism on a grade school playground, the result of multiple levels of ability interacting and seeking a mutual benefit. In an era when we are increasingly aware of bullying, cyberbullying, and shaming, this particular narrative reminds us of the myriad hidden episodes of social intelligence that are possible each day if we simply embrace the challenge of working and playing with those unlike ourselves. The enticement of unsupervised recess on the playground has always been in its propensity to yield our most promising behavior. This is a story of the rebirth of goodwill.

It is 11:00 a.m. on a sunny, tropical day mid-week at Mona Primary School in Kingston, Jamaica. The year is 1977. The school bell rings to the delight of every child, signaling what was for most the best part of the day—LUNCH TIME!! Boys and girls together bolt through the classroom doors and race toward the front gates where Fudgie, a red-skinned, middle-aged man has the challenge of vending from the rear of his hatchback, a variety of light and not particularly nutritious snacks to a swarm of grade-school kids yelling out their orders over each other.

"One bun an' cheese!" "T'ree tamarind balls and a box juice!" "One cheese crunchies!" "One nutty buddy!" "One King Kong!" "Hey Fudgie! One cornbread and a sky-juice wid nuff syrup!" We drove him crazy but he still managed to satisfy the appetites and bellies of some of the most amazingly creative children.

It took us no more than fifteen minutes for us to chow down on lunch before we invited each other to play a game of dandy-shandy (a kind of dodgeball) or rounders. These schoolyard games not only strengthened our limbs but afforded us the opportunity to become creative geniuses in our own right. Most of the time we did not have balls to play with but that did not stop us. We made our own ball from somebody's empty juice-box and stuffed it with the wrappers from all our snacks and molded the box to the optimum size, weight and shape for throwing. Perfect! Then it was time to pick teams. The girls, in their pink tunics and white blouses, congregate separately from the boys. The most remarkable thing about this process is how we always ensured that everyone who wanted to play had the chance to play regardless of skill level—and what's more, we did this all without adult supervision. The most skillful kids were designated as team captains and they selected their team members from the remaining kids, the better players getting drafted early in the process. Most of the time I remained unselected as I was not the most athletic, but that never made me the proverbial cheese that stood alone. Since everyone was granted an opportunity to participate, we agreed that I or any odd person would go first (as I would be an easy "out" in any event) and then once again every time before the teams switched sides. I am often warmed at my recollection of the sense of unity and inclusion that we practiced among ourselves in those early years at recess. It was as if we instinctively knew the importance of having everyone involved, no matter how small or great our individual talents were. The stronger ones supported the weaker and we learned what it meant to have a sense of community.

In a recent *New York Times* article about the book titled *Give and Take,* by Wharton School professor of organizational psychology Adam Grant, it quickly becomes clear that the motivating power of empathy and the happiness one stands to gain by supporting another individual is vastly underrated. Within an economic and educational environment that fosters selfish behavior and individual achievement as the primary blueprint for success, the selfish ego says, "I created mine, let him create his own." The swarm intelligence displayed in the preceding story of a day among schoolmates on a Jamaican playground offers a firm retort to the selfish ego, saying, "We were each given scaffolds, and in turn we share our scaffolds for each one to build up their own life, liberty, and happiness. Feel free to join in." Upon reflection, creativity, perhaps more than anything else, is simple generosity.

MOMENTS OF REFLECTION

This second story of swarm intelligence was sent to me from a colleague in the field of art education. Dr. Christine Ballengee Morris is a Professor in the Arts Administration, Education, and Policy Department and the American Indian Studies Coordinator for Ohio State University. Ballengee Morris has written a *vicarious narrative*, telling of a reimagined use of space, respectful of the land and its usage as envisioned by the descendants and beneficiaries of an ancient North American tribal swarm. Out of moments of reflection in a coffee shop, the story that enticed the group effort to protect lands held sacred was their shared overview anticipating a humanity that no longer oversteps its boundaries. This is a story of overcoming the monster of sacrilege.

> *It was a warm summer day and I had just come in from weeding the garden. The ringing telephone disturbed the mellow tones of the late morning so I answered it. Barbara informed me that a group of people were meeting at a coffee shop and she thought I should attend, to watch and takes notes. Since Barbara is my elder, I did not question her and did what she asked. I got cleaned up and went to the coffee shop. There were several people I knew from the university—a total of seven of us. There were two American Indians, including myself. We represented six fields. We were told*

that the Octagon Earthworks site, the portion of the larger Newark Earthworks State Memorial that has been leased by the Mound Builders Country Club since 1910, was planning to expand its country club facilities and was asking the Ohio Historical Society (the owners and lessee) permission to do so in a private meeting. The Newark Earthworks includes the remnants of the "Great Circle Earthworks, Octagon Earthworks (joined by parallel walls to another circle), and Wright Earthworks, a large, nearly perfect square enclosure."[24] Although the Newark Earthworks now contained a country club and its golf course, they are the largest set of geometric earthen enclosures in the world and were originally constructed "between 100 B.C. and A.D. 500 by a people we know today as the Hopewell Culture," likely used by these early Native Americans as "places of ceremony, social gathering, trade, and worship, and as cemeteries."[25] The coffee shop gathering was deeply concerned with the proposed expansion and its impact on this ancient archaeological site, especially the Octagon Earthworks.

The task for the next hour or so was to brainstorm ways in which this further destruction of the earthworks could be stopped. The conversations went from exploring the historical occupation, to legal and perceived illegal rights, and finally to some interesting thoughts and ideas. Each person building upon the others' ideas, one would never know that sitting at that table were some who did not like each other at all. But they were connected by their desire to save earthworks. As they continued to make connections and solidify their ideas, the conversations became loud and excited. At times, there was laughter; not that anyone was being funny but they were feeling exhilarated. After about an hour, one of the attendees stated that it was time to wrap it up and repeated the final agreed-upon ideas. The smiles said everything; they were happy with their plan. For me, this was a powerful moment. From that meeting, an ad hoc group was developed and a five-year plan was created. Ten years later, a university center was developed. Nomination for World Heritage recognition for the site has been completed and the earthworks are on the short list; in addition there are now educational tours, computer games, two educational websites, and a lecture series. The country club is still there but it is only a matter of time.[26]

FROM GARAGE EXPERIENCES TO PUBLIC ENGAGEMENTS

This third story of swarm intelligence is from a colleague with varied research interests in art education, visual culture, public pedagogy, digital technology, and curriculum theory. Dr. B. Stephen Carpenter II, a professor in the Art Education department at Pennsylvania State University, has written an *alternative narrative*, telling of the possibilities for beneficial action when those emerging from arts and scientific practices form a working alliance in response to a socio-environmental need. Carpenter tells of a collectively performed teaching and learning endeavor producing innovative and aesthetically designed water-filtering ceramic technology in order to confront the number one killer of children worldwide, unsanitary drinking water. The story that enticed this partnership between artists and scientists was the shared belief that difficult social problems are best addressed by those bringing their divergent ways of knowing the world and solving problems into a deliberate convergence, one that transforms public space into an arena for teaching and learning. This is a story of the quest for social action.

A number of years ago I began meeting with two colleagues—a civil engineer who specializes in environmental water issues and the director of a center for community-based initiatives. We met on a weekly basis in my garage to consider ways we might work together in the production and distribution of affordable point of use ceramic water filters within border communities in south Texas to respond to their need for adequate access to potable water. Informed by my background in ceramics and ongoing scholarship as an artist, I offered my home garage studio as a meeting point, outfitted with the materials and equipment to produce the filters as well as the physical space to remove ourselves from the conventional structures of the university to allow for our unconventional collective to evolve. As time progressed we each invited individuals to join us on Friday afternoons—Filter Fridays we called them. Included among the individuals we invited were undergraduate and graduate students, colleagues, local community members, teachers, and secondary students.

Over the course of almost three years, our Filter Fridays became an ever-changing collective of participants who learned the details of production and application of the filters but who also became contributors of their own knowledge and experience with affordable technologies, environmental politics, and the global water crisis among other topics. Beyond my original two colleagues and myself, there was no sense of an "official" roster of participants. Over the years, participants came and went with irregular frequency. Simply, these Filter Fridays took the form of a collective of individuals, working with, teaching, and learning from each other in a collaborative nature.

A series of public pedagogical performances have emerged from these semi-private Filter Fridays in my garage in Texas. That is, based on the collective nature of these informal, somewhat unstructured gatherings within a space designated for creative production of ceramic filters and other cultural objects, emerged the idea of "taking the show on the road" and setting up a temporary studio in public spaces in which the entire production process of the filters could take place. Similar to the idea of taking only the basic survival necessities along on a camping trip, these public pedagogical performances were equipped with only the basic materials necessary to produce point of use ceramic water filters—dry clay, sawdust, water, mixing containers, plaster molds, and on occasion a seven-foot steel ram press. The initial public performance took place on the steps in front of the university museum for an entire afternoon, attracting perhaps a hundred passers-by to stop, observe, and interact with my collaborators and myself in the production of the water filters.

Through the process of teaching the basics of clay mixing and wedging, and actual production of the filters, the public became participants in the collective process of the performance itself. The boundaries between performers and audience, performance and public, teachers and learners blurred and overlapped. Members of the public brought with them their own experiences that ranged from water issues, engineering, health, art, ceramics, and community interventions, among others.

Why do stories like these entice us so? Why do they redirect our behavior, alter our identities and become the scripts for community renewal? Ultimately, the enticement of any story at any level is in its ability to either enhance or reinforce our lived experiences. For one person, his story of a face-to-face encounter with a statue carved hundreds of years ago by the hands of Michelangelo changes his life to take the shape of a contemporary sculptor; for another, her story of childhood playground altruism still echoes today in her extraordinarily generous spirit and career in various service professions; for yet another, the oral storytellers of her Native American ancestry are honored by her story of the preservation of their sacred lands in our day and age; and for a potter, his story of the public arena as a space for the shared performance of social responsibility opens the door to the future of the human superorganism.

The enhancing and reinforcing experiences provided by stories entice us to tell them over and over again. They become tremors within our everyday lives, shattering previous boundaries, unfolding new ground, cracking the crusts of convention and tradition, and shaking away the sediment that so often obscures our civic imagination. This is why our stories so often become our touchstones, leaving those who swear by them reverberating in the midst of epiphany, clarity, or greater simplicity. Stories like these are vital to the process of individual and cultural identity formation. Stories like these leave us naked and soft and we understand who we are again—or who we are becoming for the very first time. Without the enticement of new or recurrent stories to live by, thinking rigidifies, emotions dull, culture stagnates, and development halts. The stories we live by and which populate our thinking become narrative possibilities so that "the mind is at every stage a theater of simultaneous possibilities."[27] Likewise, stories like these also become our narrative alternatives, through which we "inhabit vicariously another human being who at first seems so unlike us and yet at heart *is* like us."[28]

In summary, behave like you're part of a story—like the beloved children's literature character, Harold, and his famous purple crayon, *reinterpret everything as you go*. In the next chapter of *Swarm Intelligence*, I will attempt to reinterpret our collective public schooling effort in a way that draws upon each preceding chapter to propose an educational model fostering collaborative social networks with truly creative consequences.

CHAPTER SEVEN

SCHOOLS

TWENTY-FIRST-CENTURY CREATIVE PARTNERSHIPS AND EDUCATION WITHOUT BORDERS

In mid-March 2013, I drove four hours in a straight shot from Syracuse, New York, to State College, Pennsylvania. The weather was still so changeable that I traveled through bright sunlit hills to rain showers to snow squalls to frigid valleys. I had been asked to represent Syracuse University at an Alliance for the Arts in Research Universities symposium. This alliance first began with an invitation-only meeting on the role of art-making and the arts in research universities that was held in 2011 at the University of Michigan in Ann Arbor. It was originally assembled "to advance research and practice to enable universities to incorporate arts practices in ways that fully educate and empower…students and maximize the creative production of faculty."[1]

In that vein, one of the expected outcomes of this 2013 symposium was to "clarify research questions raised by integrated art/science/engineering research, creative work, and teaching."[2] But as I was focused on my driving and seeking distraction by listening to radio reports about thousands of dead, bloated pigs illegally dumped into a river in China and the fears expressed by Shanghai citizens about the resulting quality of drinking water supply, an unsettling question began to press urgently to mind. In the face of such problems, does art even matter? Do arts and design practices in society and their relationship to the natural laws of swarm intelligence help to provide a formula for arriving at creative solutions for our most urgent social problems? I was late departing Syracuse and rushing to make it to my destination by nightfall—and that's when it struck me at about 80 miles per hour. The answer was yes. Art and creativity both matter a great deal.

THE MORAL ARGUMENT FOR A CREATIVE SYSTEM OF EDUCATION

We really can't do this alone. Being fruitful and multiplying the significance of the human swarm requires connections from near and far. The unconnected wither; the connected gather more connections. The arts and design practices are the connective tissue of swarm intelligence. When I was a young student at the High School of Art & Design in New York City, I sometimes chose to give my art away. It is important to note how out of character this was for me. I am a methodical art maker; it takes a lot of time and to this day I am quite content if my work stays in my studio and surrounds me. I have rarely even sold my art. For me to give something that I made away, it had to strike me that someone else *needed* it more than I did. I also started writing poetry in high school for the sole reason of addressing it to friends of mine who were either down or despairing. As I reflect back, I realize that I was intentionally practicing my art as an altruistic exercise.

Our creative choices are social responses born out of social responsibility. What separates human beings from other social creatures is our altruistic intent. Art-making practices are a tangible exercise of the moral reasoning that has helped our species as a whole to survive and thrive, a means of social responsiveness and a mechanism both for personal and broader human development. Through the arts and design practices, not only do we aggregate, accommodate, and assimilate ways of thinking and doing not initially our own, but we also distribute our own thinking and doing as an influence upon others.

The arts reproduce our most advantageous choices and thinking. Each mark we make, each idea captured and shaped through a mental or handcrafted model, each act of special recognition devoted to a valued person, object, artifact, action, event or phenomenon—also presents a compelling enticement for others to do or think likewise. And whenever others do or think likewise, a way of thinking or behaving and, ultimately, a cultural pattern is thereby strengthened. If I have discovered any advantage for myself in the refinement of my perception, understanding or behavior, as such refinements are demonstrated and displayed through my creative practices it follows that each advantage gained may be shared so that it in turn becomes an advantage for those I care for.

This is the essence of altruism, and its effect can be as immediate as the simultaneous arc and redirection of a flock of starlings veering through the sky. The altruism inherent in giving my art away is not concerned with the "survival of the fittest," but rather with the "survival of the patterns" sustaining us. Hence, the arts and design in education are a much more significant endeavor than classes promoting specialized technical skills for the talented. Nor are the arts and design in education merely recreational, occupational, or therapeutic. This misses the point. The arts and design in education are primarily about the big picture moral endeavor of culture creation, not the task of mastering single brushstrokes— and are therefore absolutely central to all learning and dissemination of mutually advantageous human achievements.

Turning to the story of public education in the United States, we find a system that is as wounded as any organization I have ever encountered. Diane Ravitch is an educational historian and a former U.S. deputy education secretary who used to be an insider in the conservative think tanks who thought up the No Child Left Behind (NCLB) legislation. Ravitch has offered a great deal of very open and honest reflection on the recent tenth anniversary of the inception of NCLB. In a notable change of heart, Ravitch's ardent conclusion is that NCLB was utterly and calamitously wrong.

> We have had a full decade of No Child Left Behind, and we now know that the law has been a disaster. True, it has documented the shocking gaps in passing rates between different groups of children, but it has done nothing to change the conditions that cause those gaps. We know the gaps are there; actually, we knew about the gaps long before NCLB was passed...Many children are still left behind. We know who they are...Let's be clear about what NCLB has really accomplished: It has convinced the media and major philanthropies and Wall Street hedge

fund managers that American public education is a failure and that radical solutions are required.[3]

But as Chinua Achebe observed, if we don't like the story, let's rewrite it. Unless we chase a different story of education, nothing will change. The story of American public education and global public education is ready for a reinterpretation, an altruistic intervention. What then shall the story be? The aim of stories with morals everyone can agree with is to entice us to behave together well.

A BLUEPRINT FOR A NEW STORY OF EDUCATION: SCHOOLS WITHOUT BORDERS

Let's start with what we already know. The purpose of human creativity is to replicate successful patterns for living. If what is successful for one group is at the expense of most others, creative ideas may be considered dangerous or destructive; for example, an idea to develop and deploy a new and unexpected kind of weapon. But if what is successful to one individual or group promises to be successful to most all, a single creative idea can revolutionize all social relations; for example, an idea to develop new processes or tools for education. Success stories have long been effective enticements to creative action.

For some, the most enticing story of education has been "learning by rote." In other words, learning by doing as one is told to do. This model defines education as *a system of production*, a cause-and-effect intervention by educators into an untamed society with a focus on the control of behavior, the management of work assignments, and a mastery over the destinations of a new labor force channeled through the vast schooling interchange. In this model, schools are where blue-collar and white-collar laborers are first separated, classified, and booked for departure on designated tracks. In the early twentieth century when the principles of behaviorism and the carefully observed "scientific management" became the dominant force in education, a slew of testing and measurement protocols were introduced into schools and stringently followed so that by the twentieth century "the techniques of internal measurements had moved inside the head and gained popularity, in reference to intelligence testing especially."[4]

In the subsequent decades, other protocols for supposedly "measuring" intelligence and life potential were developed, the most famous being the IQ test, a precursor of the Scholastic Aptitude Test or SAT. The results of a single test—no matter how arbitrary the circumstances of the test, how ambiguous the possible answers a student might be given to select from, or how subjective the interpretation of their responses—was enough for many educators to assume a pupil's destiny. Although, less than altruistic, this model has been a success story to those selected for the more privileged destinations.

For others, the most enticing story of education has been "learning by doing." In other words, learning by doing as one has personally cultivated the habit of doing. This model defines education as *a system of communication*, the expression of situated knowledge about a learner's relationship with his or her social world. Each learner unfolds like a flower in a garden and reveals his or her learning to those educators facilitating growth. According to educational philosopher John Dewey, a habit is an active, insistent, and immediate expression of growth, a capacity that enables a student to learn from experience as they "retain and carry over from previous experience factors which modify subsequent activities."[5] Learned habits are formed in the process of "trying and discovering, modifying and adapting."[6]

In the winter of 2005, I took my fourth grade students on a field trip to view and interact with the Gates in New York City's Central Park, a unique site installation by conceptual artists Christo and Jeanne-Claude.[7] Over the next several weeks, my students modified this experience into small-scale adaptations, by constructing their own gateways in our art studio. The opportunity to respond to the Gates provided each student with the open space to conceptualize and visualize notions about life transitions and rites of passage that were most relevant to their own lives. The idea of "learning by doing" is the success story that launched the era of child-centered progressive education.

For still others, the most enticing story of education has been "learning through interrogation." In other words, learning by resisting what one is told to do or think by always first questioning why and seeking the alternatives. This model defines education as *a system of critique*, a form of intervention and activism rendering invisible assumptions, values, and norms visible for the sake of social transformation and individual emancipation. In the wake of the 2004 United States presidential election and the buzz of conversation about the candidates among the children and families at home and at school, I proposed the idea of having each of my fourth grade students create his or her own political cartoon. In preparation for the extended exercise of conceiving, developing, and rendering a strongly opinionated cartoon, I asked each student to name and draw a picture of an injustice in the world today, essentially asking: what could they or others do to help create a solution? Critical pedagogy is the success story and engine behind ethnic studies curricula and other emancipatory and empowering approaches to education.

Let me be quick to say that there is nothing inherently wrong with learning by being told what to do, by figuring things out for oneself, or by interrogating the reasons why we continue to do things as we do in search of ways to do them better. But wouldn't it be a more interesting story if instead of just one of those educational models prevailing over the others, any approach to learning could percolate into prominence as needed?

I propose learning by improvisation, enabled through a creative worldview, spawning *emergent* learning methodologies wherein each swarm, small or large, creates its own methodology for exploring its interests and solving the tasks at hand. The idea of improvised teaching and learning engagements and strategic risk-taking in public schools has rarely been explored and is frankly antithetical to a paradigm that emphasizes behavioral management over behaving together.[8] Youngsters are independently capable of the collective, self-organizing and adaptive behavior on display in all social swarms. Evidence of this self-organization, a diversity of knowledge, indirect collaboration, and adaptive mimicking is presented in a story shared with me by David Rufo, who is nearing the completion of his doctoral studies specializing in art education and is a fourth grade classroom teacher at an independent school located in Central New York.

One day in early March 2011, as I was preparing to attend the National Art Education Association convention in Seattle, David dropped by my office to chat. I had already visited David's classroom twice since I began teaching at Syracuse University in Fall 2007. The first time was in 2008 when David had asked me to share my artwork and children's book with his kids. I was immediately impressed by the spontaneity, flexibility, and constant engagement I saw in the interactions between students and their teachers. The mutuality of respect and the quickness of response to one another was something to behold. There was freedom in that learning space, exemplified by the lack of huge teacher's desk clogging up the lanes of activity. I encouraged David to write about the learning in his classroom, as all teachers should. While he was tentative given that he had never submitted an article for publication before at that point in time, I assured David he had plenty to write about.

In particular, David was interested in fostering the capacity for individualized creative innovation among his students, and he had asked me to share as many resources as possible on the phenomenon of self-initiated art-making in youngsters, the kinds of projects and diversions in which kids excitedly engage themselves, independent of assignments given by their well-meaning teachers. The expectations of David and his teaching partner Greg Sommer are not based on the "concept of the child as a blank slate" or "tabula rasa" advanced by English philosopher John Locke, a concept of childhood that "greatly influenced the development of public schools in the nineteenth and twentieth centuries."[9] Nor are David and Greg interested in conformity for conformity's sake. Rather, their classroom expectations are based on the phenomenon of swarm intelligence and the social origins of creativity. Their students are allowed ample opportunities to act independently, developing enticing classroom routines for the common good.

My students thrive when they have a role in constructing the structure and determining the routine. In the back of my classroom we have two carts that contain a variety of art supplies. Surrounding the carts are four folding tables. The cart area does not look like a place of structured learning; rather it appears as a wild assortment of paint, brushes, scissors, glue, markers, drop cloths, clumps of string, and torn bits of wax paper. Teachers do not manage this space, nor is it dictated by a curriculum. This space belongs to the children. There is no set agenda or protocol and the students are allowed to engage with the space as they see fit, often blurring the boundaries between art, science, and play.

During lessons that do not involve this environment, we always have one or two students who will quietly get up as if to sharpen a pencil only to segue to the back of the room and begin picking through various items in the carts. Soon another student will see this, pretend to go to the bathroom but instead make his or her way back to the art space as well. Like honeybees scouting for nesting sites, most students find a way to the carts throughout the day. Although fascinated by their self-initiated creations, I am compelled to shepherd them back to their seats in an effort to ensure they are present for the direct instruction portion of the lesson.

The conception of the youngster as an independent and critical thinker defies the typical conception of childhood thinking as so susceptible, underdeveloped, and incapable as to perpetually require the shaping hand of mature adults in place of a parent. Categorizing childhood as a state of dependency and immature thinking has made it easy to justify institutionalized public schooling practices as a permanent intervention into the supposedly unruly frontiers of childhood. However, as is the case within all swarms, collective, self-organizing and adaptive behavior requires wandering outside the boundary lines and allowing students to bring back what they find. The agency for this activity requires educators and learners without borders.

In the old story of public education, the divergent, meandering explorations and interests of learners are viewed as a deficit—it has become a blended story, one that is conflated with social pathology and a fear of the lack of mature guidance. This blended story yields a consistent misinterpretation of the capacity of youngsters, reproducing the spectacle of the delinquent child, the unregulated child, and the distracted child when children are expected to remain docile and unseen; the "heathen" child in need of assimilation at missionary and tribal schools; or the modern fable of the unruly "inner city" child in need of a savior who will lay down some tracks and straighten out that child's path.

In the new story of public education I am proposing, the blueprint going forward will be to create schools and educational programs that excel at closing the swarm intelligence gap rather than the achievement gap. Close the first gap, and the other gaps will also be shored up.

THE LAW OF SUCCESSION AND IDEAS WORTH SPREADING

Each principle in the blueprint is in accord with the natural behavioral laws that govern swarm intelligence and collective creative leadership—the Law of Succession, the Law of Separation, the Law of Alignment, and the Law of Cohesion. David Rufo continues this story with his description of unfolding acts of self-initiated activity and the learning that results as two students take the lead in diverging from the larger class group during direct instructional time:

> *After seeing my students thrive in a self-motivated setting, I decided to see what would happened if I let the students continue their creative investigations unimpeded. As expected, during our direct instruction time two students made their way to the carts. Two other students brought a few supplies back to their seats. One created patterns out of colored duct tape and the other stealthily mixed water, food coloring, and silver glitter in a paper cup. By recess, the swarm picked up in intensity. A lively group of students surrounded the carts and rummaged through the supplies, using their "free time" to essentially continue their education.*

Rather than teachers as content managers and destiny sorters, teachers and more experienced learners can be rewritten as mentors, those we chase ahead after. This could appear as something very old—like the master artists of classic studio workshops teaching apprentices the secrets of their practice. Or this could look like something very new, like the clearinghouse of short and inspiring videos of motivational talks by the roster of invited creative leaders appearing at annual nonprofit TED conferences, dedicated to "Ideas Worth Spreading." TED's original intent was to bring together thinkers and doers from the worlds of Technology, Entertainment, and Design; however, TED has greatly expanded in scope since its inception in 1984, not only in the fields of practice represented there, but in its variety of conferences and initiatives—including TED*Global*, TED*Active*, TEDBooks, the TEDFellows Program and most recently the TED-Ed video platform for sharing lessons from some of the world's greatest educators, often in collaboration with talented animators, in its outreach to new audiences.

As demonstrated in the viral impact of TED videos on the internet, individuals within a creative swarm learn to chase after those in the lead so as to foster their own adaptability and forward momentum over time. In the preceding story and in accordance with the Law of Succession in swarm intelligence, two students took the lead and two more students followed, each of his or her own volition.

THE LAW OF SEPARATION AND THE OPPORTUNITY GAP

David Rufo continues his story in the following excerpt describing the interaction between classroom learners pursuing very different material and activity interests while occupying the same workstation:

When the green paint ran out, a trio of girls began to replenish it by mixing blue and yellow. Likewise, they mixed blue and red to make purple. As they continued to experiment, they stumbled upon a pleasing array of original colors to which they decided to give names. Separately, but in the same space, another student was carefully adding drops of food coloring onto generous globs of Elmer's glue. She then added glitter and used a toothpick to mix the concoction to create a kaleidoscopic effect. A third student dyed foot-long lengths of string by soaking them in tiny vials filled with food coloring. She then fished each one out with a tool fashioned from a small piece of copper wire and set them to dry on sheets of wax paper. Seeing this, the Elmer's glue girl began to search for the vials and found them in a bin that I set aside for future science experiments.

Instead of offering students the freedom to roam and explore their divergent interests, discovering their own paths of learning, the current system of public education does exactly what it is designed to do. It contains, stratifies, and sorts learners based on perceived individual abilities and inabilities. But perception does not have to remain reality; whether you change the source concepts of your perception, or the target concepts, the resulting story must change as well. The current story of public education in the United States presumes the destinies of children, and penalizes communities less wealthy than others by closing down their schools as failures, disrupting whole communities. This story does not consider the possibility that individual ability may not fully manifest itself at all until the swarm of learners it is surrounded by arrives together at an enticing learning opportunity. In other words, the "achievement gap" is more accurately characterized as an "opportunity gap"—namely the opportunity to swarm around a story of education that views the experiences of learners as an asset rather than a fatal flaw.

But rather than continue to do this and insanely expect a different result, public schooling can be rewritten to work outside the boundaries of local models typically just across the tracks that have devolved to function either as overcrowded warehouses or as virtual penitentiaries for youngsters that general society still does not expect much from. Please note that I am advocating for swarm intelligence above all; I am not a proponent for any great reliance upon the charter school movement, which has served in general to reinforce a stratification of youngsters into hierarchical layers—namely, the few who are selected for admission into a local charter school versus the majority who will never be enrolled. As of 2013, only 6 percent of all schools in the United States were charter schools.[10]

In the preceding portion of Rufo's story and in accordance with the Law of Separation in swarm intelligence, several learners have fanned out to pursue autonomous interests and yet find themselves working and playing right beside one another, creating what comes to mind as the materials at hand interact with each individual's knowledge base and imagination. The key to unlocking the swarm intelligence of any group is in understanding how important it is *not* to compartmentalize learners from one another into separate subject area classrooms or separate age group batches—rather, all that is needed is enough maneuvering room within a swarm of learners to accommodate those who are enticed at any given moment to undertake a divergent pursuit. Those with strong skills and those with weak skills in an area of study, those with thorough preparation and well-cultivated study habits and those with little preparation, those with talents in the arts and humanities and those with talent in mathematics and the sciences—each has a crucial role to play in the very same classroom hive. Individuals within a creative swarm learn a delicate but vital social interaction—how to periodically clear out elbow room *within* what might otherwise be considered a hindering throng to work to one's own interests and liking. This creates space for oneself and all of one's mates to maneuver freely, speeding up the progress of the entire group toward its next collective learning objective.

THE LAW OF ALIGNMENT AND KHAN ACADEMY

Once the science bin was breached, the swarm picked up intensity. When a new hive is chosen, the bee scouts signal a final "buzz run"[11] that triggers a mass exodus to the new hive. Similar to a buzz run, the children quickly flipped the lids off of the remaining bins and grabbed test tubes, graduated cylinders, pipettes, and other assorted items. This sudden unorthodox use of equipment allocated for science projects made me uneasy. I worried that the materials might end up lost or destroyed. I worried that an administrator or parent might stop by and disapprove of this unconventional use of materials. But I remained steadfast in my small-scale research project and allowed the buzz to develop.

In the preceding continuation of Rufo's story and in accordance with the Law of Alignment in swarm intelligence, he describes how the enticement toward an unorthodox use of equipment generates a "buzz run," ultimately triggering the excited response of the whole classroom of learners. Likewise, schools and classrooms can be rewritten so as not to function in competition with one another for federal funding or test scores, but rather as cohorts seeking to align with other pace-setting swarms also learning to behave together. A learning community does not require containment within a brick-and-mortar or cinderblock building, especially in our contemporary digital era and information economy. An example of a school without borders is the online nonprofit Khan Academy founded by Salman Khan, a former hedge fund analyst with a wide range of interests reflected in his four college degrees in math, electrical engineering, computer science, and business.

Khan's original intent was purely altruistic—his video tutorials were a means of helping his niece remotely with her math homework. Khan soon discovered that his tutorials, first posted on YouTube, were garnering other viewers whose feedback was profuse with gratitude for the help they provided others struggling to learn basic math. Today, the Khan Academy has millions of dollars of funding support from the Bill and Melinda Gates Foundation as well as over 4 million pupils every month from all over the world, each following a series of voiceover lessons from a video library covering subjects ranging from K-12 math, biology, chemistry, physics, astronomy, finance, and the humanities.

Declaring as its mission the provision of a free, world-class education to anyone, anywhere, its intent remains philanthropic. Each playlist of instructional videos is aligned into virtual clusters based upon subject matter interest that are configured to appeal to learners who might be youngsters or adults, at home or in classrooms. Each pupil masters the materials presented on a digital chalkboard in the ten- to fifteen-minute lessons one level at a time before self-initiating graduation to the next level. Individuals within a creative swarm learn to align themselves in finely knit affinity group attachments or communities of practice based on an altruistic give-and-take preserving the fabric of the larger group of digital learners. In the Khan Academy, education takes place in a school without borders.

THE LAW OF COHESION AND FINLAND'S EDUCATIONAL REVOLUTION

By the end of the day, the girl who was dyeing string decided to integrate her idea into a science fair experiment. The group of students who were mixing their own hues ended up bottling samples to sell online under the name Professor Paints. The girl who had first found the vials continued to explore their aesthetic potentials by adding objects to the food coloring: tiny spirals of wire, bits of pencil eraser, and a dusting of glitter. She ended up creating a series of diaphanous works that were at once strange and sublime.

Every day I am torn between allowing the students to go to the carts when they feel inspired to create and making sure they remain seated in order to get the assigned classwork completed. Creative ways of thinking do not align with standardization or predetermined outcomes.... According to author Peter Miller, when there is a "controlled messiness...the wisdom of the hive emerges."[12] Self-initiated experiences allow each student to indulge in his or her own project while also promoting a creative environment that benefits the whole classroom.

In this final passage from Rufo's story of classroom learning and in accordance with the Law of Cohesion in swarm intelligence, we view a learning community pursuing an environment that is beneficial to all. To complete a new blueprint for public education, instructional goals and policies must be rewritten to facilitate "learning by behaving together," evidenced by cooperative creative achievements. In the nation of Finland, this kind of blueprint for public education has been adopted as a working model for the last 30 years. In fact, in Finland all education is public education—there is no option but to accept the responsibility to behave in such a way that prevents any citizen and their contribution to the group from getting lost or overlooked along the way.

Only a small number of independent schools exist in Finland, and even they are all publicly financed. None is allowed to charge tuition fees. There are no private universities, either. This means that practically every person in Finland attends public school, whether for pre-K or a Ph.D.[13]

More importantly, public education in Finland has become a globally acknowledged success story, ranking at or near the top in reading, math, and science in every significant global survey of developed countries since the year 2000. The fruit of ongoing efforts to reform Finnish education since the 1980s "has led to a continuous stream of foreign delegations making the pilgrimage to Finland to visit schools and talk with the nation's education experts, and constant coverage in the worldwide media marveling at the Finnish miracle."[14] What story of education has provided Finland's schooling blueprint?

It all begins with the Law of Cohesion. Finnish society is committed to "the idea that every child should have exactly the same opportunity to learn, regardless of family background, income, or geographic location."[15] In Finland's story of education, the cultivation of star performers and the competition for individual achievement scores is secondary to converging toward a point in time when the structures of social inequality cannot be sustained. But in its focus on equity—valuing shared responsibility over accountability and creative play over cramming for tests—Finland has *also* achieved excellence.

While Americans obsess over questions like, "How can you keep track of students' performance if you don't test them constantly?," in Finland there are no standardized tests except for the National Matriculation Exam administered at the end of the Finnish equivalent to high school at around the age of eighteen. Teachers simply accept the responsibility "to assess children in classrooms using independent tests they create themselves."[16] In fact, there is no word in the Finnish language that corresponds to the word "accountability." According to Pasi Sahlberg, director of the Finnish Ministry of Education's Center for International Mobility and the author of a new book on the lessons the world can learn from the success of Finland's education reforms, "Accountability is something that is left when responsibility has been subtracted."[17] There is no need to constantly test youngsters and to condition teachers to focus classroom instructional time only on content that will increase the likelihood of students passing those tests if teachers are trusted to do what they are paid to do. The story of public education in Finland tells of a highly respected and well-paying occupation. Teacher training programs are highly selective and a master's degree is required to enter the profession.

It should not be surprising at all that when the responsibility for the success of a classroom of students is fully entrusted to their teachers, rather than to politically motivated or austerity-driven accountability measures, it leads to more excellent teaching and learning practices. In a popular RSA Animate YouTube video illustrating a talk by author Daniel Pink, we see that monetary rewards and penalties make poor motivators for top performance.[18] Numerous experiments by psychologists, sociologists and economists alike all indicate that when it comes to tasks and assignments requiring more than rudimentary cognitive skills to accomplish, the three factors that lead to the best performance results are: creative autonomy; the intrinsic drive to get better at a task and ultimately to master it; and a sense of larger purpose beyond the task at hand that works in concert with a pattern of social behavior offering mutual benefit to the entire swarm. If all educators were allowed similar opportunities for professional autonomy, the galvanization of daily challenges, and the pursuit of greater creative purpose, their natural adherence to the intelligence of the Law of Cohesion would manifest better schooling practices and outcomes than we can currently imagine.

In summary, behave like you're part of a school of thought—*teach and learn without borders, practicing a story of autonomous creation, which later transitions to mastery, mentorship, and the achievement of greater social purpose.*

CHAPTER EIGHT

RETHINKING CREATIVITY

THE HABITS AND PRINCIPLES OF INNOVATION

The planet's honeybee colonies are dying off at an accelerating rate and the implications are probably more serious than you realize. According the U.S. Department of Agriculture, a quarter of the American diet relies on pollination from honeybees and yet because of some mysterious malady to date we have lost 40 to 50 percent of this nation's hives.[1] The list of fruit and vegetable crops that would not flourish without the pollination services of honeybee hives is extensive, including "apples, cucumbers, broccoli, onions, pumpkins, carrots, avocados, almonds."[2] The increasing possibility of the extinction of honeybees is likely the result of a calamitous cocktail of interacting pesticides and fungicides, invasive parasitic mites, and other factors affecting the bees' food supply and immune systems. No one is exactly sure of the cause just yet, but the crisis cannot be ignored and is undergoing intensive scientific study. Most noteworthy to the story of swarm intelligence is the fact that the pollination of our food crops is a natural byproduct of a honeybee's hunt for food sources for the hive. Likewise, creativity is the natural byproduct of swarm intelligence.

At the start of this book, I began by addressing two simultaneous questions. First, I asked: "Where is creativity located?" Over the course of this writing it has become apparent that creativity is an incubating continuum, a social reservoir of genius that individuals tap into, feed upon, and refine. Secondly, I asked: "Why does creativity matter?" It is clearer now that creativity matters because it is how we human beings enrich and extend our social and intellectual gene pool from generation to generation. Procreation is not just a matter of producing offspring; humanity also reproduces its best and most durable ideas. Hence, my creativity is not like your creativity. Creative learners and workers first process and then share their acquired advantage like worker bees regurgitating the collected nectar of flowers in the form of honey for all. In the same way that no bee colony's honey tastes exactly the same, my creativity has its own lineage; so does yours.

It is now time to revisit the question, "What is creativity?" In so doing, this book now turns its attention toward advocacy for new approaches to fostering innovation and creativity in both business and education. What if we began to rethink creativity as more of a systemic phenomenon than an individual trait, a social form of intelligence that activates the latent culture-making potential of everyone involved?

MY CREATIVE LINEAGE, YOUR CREATIVE LINEAGE

My father was a stubborn man. Like most other men, especially those married with children, he wanted to make a living that would support his family. He was born and raised in the neighborhood of Brownsville, in Brooklyn, a borough of New York City. His was a stubbornness that reminds me of images of the clean white rectangular placards associated with the Memphis Sanitation Workers Strike of 1968, each sign positioned in front of the chest of an African American laborer, printed with the declaration "I Am A Man" in ultra-large, expertly printed black letters. Black men carried those signs during that strike because the dominant society had a tendency to misread them as something other than equal citizens. In reality, these workers simply wanted to make a fair living. They were not lazy. And they were not invisible. Their signage was a brief narration of the history of labor relations in the United States with the working poor, both slave and free, yet commonly devalued as individuals of lesser value to society and unworthy of consideration by those in power. The aspirations of these laborers went unnoticed until asserted.

My father wanted to be visible and make his living *as an artist*, a story unheard of in the neighborhood he grew up in. My father—an African American who came into his manhood at the start of the Civil Rights era—became a product designer, children's book author, art director, typographer, advertiser, and freelance artist (see Figure 2). Creating this identity from nothing was an example of identity as work of art—it introduced a narrative into my lifeworld that continues to inform my own discourse on the relevance of the arts in education. The narrative is this: creation is power. Creation requires the acquisition of resources,

Figure 2 Portrait of me as a boy with a mind full of connections, as painted by my father

converting them into benefits. As I grew older, I realized that all of this resource acquisition had made me a scholar—and that's when I realized that one of the secrets to exceling in education and citizenship was in learning how never to stop being creative.

I understood my creative lineage early. This probably contributed to my being tracked as gifted and talented throughout the early part of my K-12 education. However, I would argue that I was not more "gifted" than the average child. To my mind, there were way too many things most other kids were good at—things

I clearly had little aptitude for. What I did have was *curiosity*, a genuine openness to taking on and self-sustaining a new interest. I rarely said of a schooling activity, *"This is not for me."* And you could rarely bore me in school because I had a knack for finding the aspects in any material presented to me that I did not know before. Frankly, all I really wanted of a learning engagement was the pleasurable notion of expanding my thinking just by adding a few new pieces. So if you ever saw me engaged in the odd habit of reading a dictionary or encyclopedia, it was because I knew it was time to fill my pollen basket and reenergize.

The assertion of a life narrative is a form of power, but not just in the sense of the personal agency afforded. Life narratives are an energy source, the pollinators of our creative lineages—the greater the variety of cross-pollinating narratives, the richer, more plentiful, and capacious the fields of our dreams. Students and employees in general society do not need teachers and managers holding their hands to help them intuit what aspects of contemporary culture they will make the most use of. The work of making useful sense of the life stories that might be incorporated into their intellects has already been done, and will continue to be done, without our aid as creative leaders. Nevertheless, those of us who have already assumed any form of leadership do have a crucial part to play. Our task requires nothing short of a complete rethinking of the role of curriculum both in education and in workplace training and professional development.

Because creativity is a continuum, we cannot teach people to be creative. However, it is not because some people are creative and most people are not; as has already been established throughout this book, that notion is a harmful myth. No matter how creative I am, I cannot teach you to be creative for the simple reason that my creativity is different from your creativity. Just as no one's child looks and behaves exactly the same as anyone else's child in the nation, my creativity will also look and behave differently because my creative lineage differs from yours. That is why portrait artists create differently than architects who create differently than business entrepreneurs who create differently than novelists, or athletes, or singers, or heart surgeons, or parents, or police detectives. And this would be common sense except for the fact that the existing paradigm of who is creative and who is not is more powerful than we realize, masking the creative achievements that take place right in front of our eyes each and every day.

Rather than attempting to replicate my exact approach to creativity within someone else's thinking, all that is necessary is that creative leaders provide multiple access points to the creative social continuum—that we remove the workbooks with preselected answers, unblock the windows and doors, distribute some useful tools, and demonstrate some of our own successful routines. When we allow students and employees to build their own gateways of interest, to select their own resources and affiliations, and to trample their own pathways toward a selected creative practice, they will find a way. As creative leaders, we are not only obligated to get out of the way—we are also then obligated to invite creative learners back in to camp to show us the way to their road less traveled. There will be so much for us all to learn in the process. On this journey, no one's story of creativity is supposed to be exactly the same as the next wayfarer's. That is not the way stories are supposed to work anyhow. Stories only take us near to where they are projected to lead us, not precisely to where we want to go.

Curriculum is also a continuum. It is not located in a work-book. Curriculum theorist William F. Pinar argues that the reconceptualization of curriculum begins with the subjective lessons of autobiographical experience.[3] Similar to the telling of a life story, the journey toward creative awareness and practice in contemporary society is necessarily complicated by a mess of plausible starting points and ending points. Patrick Slattery suggests a reconceptualization of curriculum that extends its map far outside the boundaries of the typical classroom or workplace learning when he writes the following:

> [T]he verb form of curriculum, *currere*...refers to the running of the race rather than the race course itself....This process view of curriculum as *currere*...emphasizes the individual's own capacity to reconceptualize his or her autobiography, recognize connections with other people, recover and reconstitute the past, imagine and create possibilities for the future, and come to a greater personal and communal awareness....From this postmodern perspective, the curriculum as *currere* is an interpretation of lived experiences rather than a static course of studies to be completed.[4]

Within the continuum of lived experiences, learning to be creative is the study of alternatives. Individual choices will be made, and then be made meaningful as an enticement for others also to elect if they choose to do so. Creativity is therefore a meaning-making behavior; it is a lifelong study, honeycombed with inherited and adopted creative lineages, ultimately superseding anything that can be taught in a classroom or a training session. For where creativity is concerned, autobiography matters.

PERSONAL KNOWLEDGE WITHIN THE SOCIAL ARCHITECTURE OF CREATIVITY

As I was writing this chapter, a student shared a small black-and-white cartoon with me, a drawing of a youngster sitting with his teacher at a round table in an elementary school classroom explaining, "I don't think I can express what I have to say in just colored paper and glue." The child's pronouncement is akin to a notion about creativity that comes to us from the scientist and philosopher Michael Polanyi, author of books such as *Personal Knowledge* and *The Tacit Dimension*. Polanyi urges readers to recognize that we each start from the same position as it relates to making meaning from life experience, the fact that *"we can know more than we can tell."*[5] The fact that our interface with the tacit knowledge of personal life experiences serves as a wellspring for all of our most enticing stories heightens the relevance of Brent Wilson's conception of creative research and practice "as *re-search*, to search again, to take a closer second look," implying an ongoing search for evidence "about the way things were in the past, how they are presently, and even about how they might be in the future."[6]

Creativity in practice cannot be limited in conception as referring only to a work of art or design because the amplitude of a single idea may be revisited across a number of modalities within the life of its creator(s)—re-searched over and again in written words, images, actions, conversations and public talks, products, team projects or even business models. Over time, the creator(s) may pick up any previously wrought outcome or interpretation and recast it, either in part or as a whole—similar to using in-text citations and quotes from prior publications in new manuscripts, or the technique of "sampling" digitally encoded melodic riffs or lyrical phrases from old recorded songs in the composition of new music.

Two of the most creative business entrepreneurs of our time—Steve Jobs of Apple and Bill Gates of Microsoft—working in collaboration with their respective research and design teams, have generated whole product lines born from the finely calibrated practice of taking a closer, second look at internal creative lineages. Apple and Microsoft made improvements along the way, each continually adding a new product or feature as it became needed to fill a gap in the ongoing story of their brand's usefulness to its consumer base. In doing so, Apple and Microsoft became two of the most successful businesses in the world. As a life practice, creativity reinvents itself.

In its perpetual state of reinvention, creative research and practice leaves behind trail markers, residual signs of intellectual passage, often in aesthetically satisfying formats replete with elements that express their meanings only in relation to all the other elements represented "in a dense, continuous field."[7] Works of visual art and poetry have long been trail markers of my personal store of knowledge along the continuum of study I continue to travel in and out of school, in and out of workplace environments.

The earliest manifestations of my creative lineage appeared in a modest two-story brick home at 1260 Lincoln Place in Brooklyn. My father, Jim Rolling, was a professional artist and always kept one room as his art studio. My own course of study began as I first taught myself to draw in this art studio, referencing superhero stories from my father's collections of Marvel and DC comic books, the odd and alienated characters created by illustrator

Charles Addams, original paperback printings of Charles Schulz's *Peanuts* cartoon anthologies, and the science fiction of television shows like *The Six Million Dollar Man* and *The Incredible Hulk*. I learned to generate self-initiated narratives of possibility using my father's art supplies as needed.

My familiarity with the power of self-initiated narratives as a source of creative identity led directly to the "Who I Am" project, one of my final curricular contributions to the children I worked with daily as a lead K-4 visual arts teacher for an elementary school in New York City before starting my new job as an Assistant Professor at Penn State University. The project I proposed was a follow-up to a field trip with all three third grade classes to New York City's El Museo del Barrio in March 2005 to view an exhibition of personal knowledge titled *Retratos: 2000 Years of Latin American Portraits*. One of the striking features of this traveling collection of portraits was how many markers of personal and political identity were physically embedded in, inscribed, or otherwise represented upon the surfaces of the displayed artifacts as touchstones of memory, passed down from generation to generation in the form of family heirlooms. Back in the art classroom following the exhibition, we began to discuss the questions: "What is an heirloom?" "Is it valuable to the family because it is expensive, or are there more personal reasons for its significance?"

Unfortunately, the difficult logistics of arranging this trip pushed it back to a particularly busy time of the school year as we were approaching both Spring Recess and the end of the second trimester. So we revisited the inquiry on heirlooms and personal knowledge during our Integrated Projects Week, or IPW, at the close of the final trimester. An IPW was intended to involve small groups of students from different classes and grade levels in a focused and extended collaborative learning exercise. The self-selection of IPW inquiry projects allowed each student to make his or her own choices—deepening each one's understanding of a chosen topic, theme, or concept already encountered in the curriculum in order for enrollees to further pursue their interest. Final projects were then exhibited and/or performed in a culminating school-wide showcase to which all families were invited.

So it came to pass that at the end of the 2004–2005 school year, I proposed the "Who I Am" storytelling project, wherein family artifacts, heirlooms, and personal knowledge were to serve as the inspiration for art-making, historical research, and the performance of self-image and family identity. A kindergarten teacher named Mr. Johns assisted me. The students who chose to participate in the "Who I Am" project were required to bring home a letter introducing the important notion of children relating family stories, while transforming meaningful personal knowledge and family heirlooms into creative works as an exploration of personal identity.

To inaugurate the "Who I Am" project, I gathered the participating students into an empty classroom. We sat down on a rug in a storytelling circle with a few learning objects on hand. First, I introduced *1260 Lincoln Place*, a mixed-media representation of my experience of the home I grew up in. It incorporates a life-sized self-portrait, along with a portrait of my younger brother Dwayne, both of us visible in my childhood bedroom window. Each brick on the face of the exterior wall was handcrafted and placed askew; the figures of my brother and I were molded out of soil and clay. The careful modeling of the facial features was colored with layer upon layer of oil pastels. The shirts worn by the two figures were cut from the rags of shirts we actually wore as children. The original working venetian blinds were actually taken from my old bedroom window. The print of the youngster playing baseball was a one-generation old heirloom passed down to us; it was once hung on my father's bedroom wall when he himself was a boy and was valuable for no other reason. The entire piece was too heavy to be physically passed around the storytelling circle as an object, so my students were invited to step forward and touch the bricks and faces depicted in the artwork, as well as to raise and lower the blinds.

This first learning object was then juxtaposed with some very old photographs that I subsequently passed around; the photographs belonged to the family albums of my friend Pam. I first met Dr. Pamela Harris Lawton when we were both students of art education in the same doctoral cohort at Teachers College, Columbia University. She is currently a member of the faculty and Director of Education Studies at the Corcoran College of Art+Design. Like me, Pam is also a studio artist and arts-based researcher. Pam describes her effort to condense family stories, records and photographs into visual/verbal art artifacts of her creative lineage that were accessible and easy to read. She writes: "I wanted to create visual documents that could be circulated, used to teach family history to the young, and yet be so aesthetically pleasing that instead of being filed safely away in a trunk, drawer or closet, they could be displayed as works of art in the homes of family members where inquisitive young minds and eyes could seek them out and ask questions."[8]

As I was conceiving the "Who I Am" project, I recalled viewing one such work of art exhibited by Pam several years prior at Teachers College, a story based upon her rescue of a family heirloom—a compact folding portable desk invented in the early 1940s by one of her recent ancestors, an accomplished architectural modelmaker and dollhouse designer named James W. Butcher. The original photographs and copies of newspaper articles that Pam was kind enough to send me included photos of the heirloom in disrepair upon initial discovery and retrieval from some attic, basement, or closet. The portable desk was then photographed once again after the loving act of re-search, restoration, and story-telling orchestrated by Pam as she transformed the once-forgotten heirloom into a work of art. Regarding the portable desk and her reclamation of the legacy of her "Papa Will" (as Mr. Butcher was affectionately called among family members), Pam writes: "Papa Will used wallpaper to decorate the sides of his desks. I peeled off the wallpaper and in place of it collaged prints and photocopies of photos and documents telling the story of Papa Will's life on the outside panels of the desk. And then because he was so involved in making things by hand, I had the idea of sculpting in clay a replica of his hands in the act of sketching ideas for future wood-working projects—in effect putting him into the piece."[9]

After viewing both my work and Pam's juxtaposed and handling all of the learning objects with care, the children in the storytelling circle were asked to draw upon their own life stories to make some connections of their own. What heirloom from their home would they each like to ask permission from their parents to bring to class and transform into a creative work? The students considered the possibilities with much enthusiasm; each child was given a sketchbook and asked to mark out some preliminary ideas for their projects as they came to mind.

Nyasa, one of my third grade students, saw the possibilities in the creative exploration of her great grandmother's childhood long ago on the Caribbean island of Barbados, as compared to her own childhood in the present-day United States. The opportunity to make art in her elementary school classroom was stimulated with a simple and precious family heirloom—a jar of sand carried away from the beaches of Barbados when her great grandmother just before she immigrated to these shores. As she meandered through the many possible creative explorations, Nyasa found a connection that made sense to her, a story she knew that was worth telling through a series of clay figurines, a story of the passage of time and the passing down of created meaning from one generation to the next. I asked all my students to write about the significance of the idea revisited through their art-making:

> My great grandmother came to this country with her two children and a jar of sand with her from the beach. She brought the sand with her as a reminder of Barbados. The sand is a piece of her country [and] it also represents if we can't be in Barbados, it will be with us.... I began with the sand and thought about what I was going to do. I got the idea of making a timeline to show how the sand got passed down the family tree.... I got the idea of using clay people to symbolize my family, giving the sand to one another. I put my great grandmother and my grandmother in the first box, my grandmother and mother in the second box and my mother and me in the third box.... I got the idea of making it three-dimensional because I thought it would be weird if it was on paper. I also got the idea of how I want to tell the story.[10]

This was Nyasa's story, her own curriculum creation. Her home-room class had been studying timelines and family trees during the recent school year; as her art teacher, I had not been studying these things and any suggestions I might have offered drawn from my own personal knowledge would have led Nyasa in other directions. Fortunately, I had purposed to let the students initiate their own directions, make their own meanings, and to be on hand primarily to facilitate their constructions.

Shiva, one of my fourth grade students during the "Who I Am" project, was allowed to bend the rules a bit and literally chose his passport as the heirloom around which to build a work of art. Although the passport itself had not been passed down from generation to generation, the *principle* of owning a personal passport was in fact a most authentic and powerful inheritance. Shiva explains:

This passport is important because it shows my personal information and allows me to travel. With my passport I can go to different states and countries. With my passport I can also see new things, visit new places and meet new people. In these places I can find out how they live, why they like the way they live and what is important to them. When I see new things and monuments I ask myself questions such as why it was made, who made it and how old it is. I got my passport when I was 6 months old and it will expire in 2008. My first trip was a trip to India. I visit India every year to see my family. I have a large family. I wouldn't know many of them without my passport. Without this passport I would not have realized how lucky I am because some people do not have lucky lives. Some people don't have good schools, some children are working and there are all these other problems like world poverty and dirty hospitals. I consider myself lucky.[11]

In the case of fourth grade student Dustin, his joy was palpable as he saw his great-grandmother for the very first time. Dustin's personal family artifact was a green beret that first belonged to his great-grandmother, was passed down to his father, and then given to Dustin. According to Dustin, his great-grandmother Adda Bozeman spoke at military academies during the Vietnam War era and was an advocate in favor of the effectiveness of human intelligence over too great a reliance upon satellite surveillance in the practice of espionage. The green beret was apparently a gift to Dr. Bozeman in connection with one of these speeches. This was all that Dustin knew. He told me he had never seen a photograph of his great-grandmother before.

I proceeded to help Dustin do a quick online search for his great-grandmother's name and we found out that she had been a Professor of International Relations at Sarah Lawrence College. Moreover, we discovered that the Sarah Lawrence College Archives had photographs of Dr. Bozeman in her role as an educator. I made an urgent request for digital copies of these photos on behalf of Dustin so that he could incorporate them into his project. Given the tight timeline, it was to our delight that our request was granted. For Dustin, receiving these photographs of a family member he had never met or seen was like uncovering buried treasure. His parents had never seen these particular photos either, so Dustin was able to forward the images home as a gift, to his father especially.

Tal, one of my third graders, was in the unique position of being a student in my regular-day art classroom twice a week. He had elected to sign up for my afterschool portrait-making class and the additional week-long "Who I Am" IPW offering. In the following previously published correspondence offered by Tal's mother, who was a research psychiatrist at a New York City hospital at the time, she introduces her son as an emerging creative identity:

I have a wonderful son named Tal (age 9) who has many talents. However, fine motor control and visual perception were not two of them. As a child, he never drew—ever. It was unclear whether this was due to lack of interest, lack of skill, or some combination of the two. His passion was baseball, and you didn't need to draw to play shortstop. As a result, when he told me one day that his only complaint with his new school was that he did not have enough art time I was startled. Even more startling was when he signed up for "Master Portrait Drawing" as an afterschool class. He chose this class even though it required attendance twice a week for 2 hour sessions each, and it prevented him from playing afterschool basketball with his best friend. I kept my mouth shut as he filled out the afterschool form, but I wondered if he would even last one week. In fact, he lasted all semester, he chose an extra week of art at the end of the school year, and he lamented the fact that his teacher was moving away and would not be at school the following year. For the first time in his life, Tal liked drawing and looked forward to art class.[12]

Why would a self-described sports enthusiast who brought his baseball glove to school each day and expressed almost no interest in art before the third grade take a curricular path so seemingly at odds with his previous journey? It was because, through my art class, Tal had tapped into the creative continuum and had found it to be beneficial. Tal's mother followed her son's development closely that semester and noticed several things that were out of the ordinary for him, things that appeared to her trained eyes to be attributable to his tapping into creativity in a way that was entirely new to him.

> *The first thing I noticed as Tal worked week after week on his family portraits was that he began to notice visual details in the external world. Historically, this was a child who struggled to discern E from F or to find something in the refrigerator right in front of him.... The second thing I noticed was his increasing ability to see both the forest and the trees. Historically, Tal had a tendency toward tunnel-vision: when he noticed a detail, he saw nothing else. He could get caught on one word in a sentence and miss the overall meaning. However, in art class, Tal was learning how to draw his brother's face, which required that he draw his brother's two eyes, nose, mouth and teeth all in the right proportion to each other. Then, he drew his mother's eyes in his mother's face, his father's ears on his father's head, etc. To make his family portraits look like his family, Tal had to move back and forth between the forest (i.e., the overall effect) and the trees (i.e., the specific facial features). I began to notice his increasing ability to do this not only with his drawing but with his thinking as well. Whether drawing taught him to do this or whether he was ready to do this and drawing was a way to practice combining the part with the whole, I don't know. However, the growth in his conceptual flexibility was quite dramatic.[13]*

Beyond all of these things, Tal had found an ability to tell new stories, filling in the gaps of his personal knowledge as he figured out his own creative identity. Tal's heirloom for the "Who I Am" project was a book from which his name was taken, titled *TAL, His Marvelous Adventures with Noom-Zor-Noom* (1929), by author

Paul Fenimore Cooper, the great-grandson of the renowned early American novelist James Fenimore Cooper. Tal did not want to permanently affix this book into a work of art so he instead chose to make a small bookshelf made out of some thick corrugated cardboard we had tucked away in one of the art studio storage closets. Tal writes about his name, his family and his "being here" in the following excerpt of his in-class writing:

> *When my mom was a kid her third grade teacher read her the book "Tal," she thought it was such a great and mysterious book. The only other person my mom knew who read the book outside of her class was her sister Lisa who had the same teacher when she was in third grade. Years later my mom met my dad. He also knew the book "Tal" because his uncle [Paul Fenimore Cooper] wrote the book. One of the earliest presents from my dad to my mom was the book "Tal"! My dad went to an out-of-print book shop, and found the book "Tal" and he gave it to my mom. They decided upon Tal as my name because they both loved the book. But in the book the boy named Tal actually had blond hair and blue eyes. I have dark hair and brown eyes.*[14]

The book was not the only object in Tal's trail-marking site installation; he also added several other exemplars of his identity in this telling. Incorporated into his bookshelf, Tal included a baseball; a second heirloom, his baseball glove, which first belonged to his father and was passed on to Tal; a clay jaguar, Tal's favorite animal, made specifically for placement within the installation; a rolled paper "chessboard" hand-ruled and hand-inked by Tal, a replication of the soft vinyl chessboards favored by the school-sponsored chess program he participated in; a copy of the front cover end paper of the book written by his father's uncle, so richly inked by the book's illustrator, Ruth Reeves, that Tal glued it onto the lower shelf of his installation; other poetry and narratives written for the occasion; and a family photograph of Tal, his little brother and parents, glued to a small picture frame constructed by Tal, and set atop the completed bookshelf.

Philosopher David Novitz has suggested that our individual and social identities are like works of art, containing "an imaginatively produced narrative core" and "constructed with a possible audience in mind."[15] In other words, we construct our life stories to be entered into the continuum of creativity. No matter how improvised our cultural identities may be, or how many interpersonal experiences commingle, the stories of these identities and experiences *already* comprise the lifeworlds of the next generation of creative leaders. But unless these new stories are continually introduced into the conversation, how will we know them?

In order to rethink creativity as the feeding trough of our next best humanity, it is important to carefully consider the creation of narrative avenues in and out of the creative continuum. The threshold to this continuum is best penetrated by new stories. And new creative leaders become unmistakably apparent when we recognize our own lived experiences—or the allure of experiences that stir us fully awake and desirous—brought to life in their creative practices.

HABITS OF INNOVATION TOWARD RENEWED CREATIVE LEADERSHIP

A habit involves repetitive movement, so ingrained in the somatic, or bodily, memory it has become an intuitive choice. Foreseeably, certain habits are crucial to swarm intelligence, a social behavior generating shifts in forward momentum so rapidly there is typically no time to think about the next move ahead. John Dewey has argued that human character would not exist if each habit "existed in an insulated compartment and operated without affecting or being affected" by the interpenetration of other habits.[16] In other words, human character is like an unbounded area of concatenating ripples as habits interact with each other like the percolations of a great lake's surface in a driving summer rain. The interpenetration of individually acquired habits of innovation and sundry avenues for repeating those behaviors ultimately cultivates a powerful "continuum of habits in terms of the [learning] environments we create."[17] According to Dewey, the acquisition of new habits of mind is perpetuated by continually unsettling prior habits through the introduction of novelties. The constant introduction of novel symbol systems, accessible tools, cultural interfaces, and/or social networks for learning and doing business generate new *impulses* that Dewey describes as the agencies of change, "giving new direction to old habits and changing their quality."[18]

The creative continuum is a system comprised of human agents, practicing beneficial habits and drawing upon experiential stories ever in flux. The local cross-current of these behavioral patterns and habits of mind found within any corner of our continuum enable it to absorb and assimilate both the anomalous and the anonymous, the sacred and the profane, the living story and the latent possibility. Living in a global churn of social contexts generates an even larger continuum of reinterpretive possibilities in the exercise of creative identity formation. In this way the creative continuum enables an individual to transcend the limitations of being an individual. Based on the preceding exploration of how to rethink creativity, here I sketch out some guiding habits for proliferating more creative education and business practices. Within a creative continuum, innovation and invention is always closer than you realize.

Creative education and business practices make a habit of requiring an "expanded pedagogy,"[19] extending far beyond the limited context of school classrooms and business boardrooms and think tanks. Expanded approaches to developing creative agency also expand the delta of story tributaries that feed an individual's creative lineage so as to incorporate social, political, and spiritual experiences from the lives of other creators in a community of practice. Community involves both the extension of personal knowledge into the local commons, and the incorporation of external sites of story content into the psyche and experience of an emerging creative leader. In so doing, the curriculum for living is expanded.

Creative education and business practices make a habit of favoring no single template of what constitutes a successful education or business model. Within the creative continuum, canons of exemplary achievement will often collide and creative models are as relative as life experiences. The creative continuum will canonize an innovative way of thinking and doing one day and then celebrate a new model of creative genius in the world on the next day—all this while working to preserve all pinnacles of creative achievement in one common skyline. The creative continuum features sheltering stories built from the imaginations and experiences of its emerging leaders. It is a metropolis where all are welcome to enter and trade.

Exemplary creative education and business practices make a habit of seeking opportunities to reinvent the creative continuum through innovations supplanting the known terrain of stories with the not-yet-known. Educational and business initiatives that seek to revisit and reinterpret the status quo recognize that any presentation of creativity as somehow isolated from the diverse sociocultural experiences we are steeped in every day fails to fully value the bazaar of lifeworlds that constitute the human condition. On the contrary, truly creative initiatives actively utilize a crosshatching of influences, redrawing the known world through narratives and blended stories heretofore unconsidered.

An effective navigation of humanity's creative continuum makes a habit of recognizing that new creative ventures are constructed upon the foundations of prior narrative structures, sometimes obscuring them, sometimes adhering to them, sometimes adapting them—but, given the advantages of a continuous creative practice, never avoiding them. Within a continuum, creative outcomes are never authored and initiated solely through a single creative agent; rather, creativity is transactional.[20] The creative continuum is co-constructed by everyone in the community of educational or business practice who likewise attempts to synthesize a collective sense of the way forward along the creative journey.

The ongoing renewal of our creative continuum requires the habit of synthesizing all that encroaches upon an individual's familiar borders—making meaning from our relationships and clashes with our material, biological, sociocultural, geological, geographical, climatic, and psychic worlds. Revisited and reinterpreted meaning is the stuff of ritual and communal remembrance. For example, using a place-based and architectural metaphor suitable for the curricular journey, elements within the creative continuum can be engaged with equal aesthetic power whether we are returning again to the Yosemite Valley, to Stonehenge, to St. Patrick's Cathedral, to the Louvre, to Fallingwater, to the Guggenheim Museum in Bilbao, or to any one of the spontaneous shrines of remembrance that sprang up on the walls, streetscapes, and sidewalks of Manhattan in the wake of the 9/11 terrorist attacks. All that lends substance to new, revisited, or reinterpreted meaning becomes an asset to the entire creative community.

Finally, creative education and business practices make a habit of affording students the opportunity to reinterpret "identity," "home," and "community" by re-presenting meaningful stories near and dear to their own lives yet invisible to others—prompting others to also journey toward familiarity with those new alternatives to the way that everyday life has previously been experienced. Our creative continuum reconstitutes itself by inviting, and sometimes demanding, each contributor to make a way even when there is no way.

THE SECRET TO INNOVATION IS YOU

In the end, the greatest secret to developing habits of innovation is neither within you nor outside of you—it *is* you. Try this: walk into a room full of people. Whatever the interpersonal dynamics before you entered has now changed. Now exit. The dynamics while you were in the midst of the room full of people changes yet again as soon as you walk out the door. You were once the missing variable and now you are the one changing variable in the experience of all involved. In each instance, you changed everything in a moment.

Likewise, swarm intelligence evolves swiftly. A behavior wherein each individual within a group is intuitively chasing ahead, separating from the crowd, aligning with the pacesetters, and converging upon a new and beneficial target requires habits of mind that have already been honed. Animals do not need common stories to chase after; trail markers laced with chemical pheromones and powerful responses to other sensory stimuli suffice as the target or motivator for creatures with lesser cerebral cortexes and more poorly developed neural networks. Instincts alone will drive the swarm forward.

Human beings are different. We distinguish ourselves from other creatures on this planet by our propensity to chase after stimuli held entirely in mind. We develop the habit of chasing after stories that entice and motivate us. We chase after the emotions that resonate with our personal temperament. We chase after aesthetic responses to what we each consider to be beautiful. We chase after nagging questions and unrelenting curiosity. We chase after justice and empathy for those in greater need than we are. We chase after the raw expression of our own humanity in written or spoken word, musical performance, and choreographed movement. We chase after our own dreams and our most ardent desires. We chase after inspiration and novel ideas—which is the likely reason you have just read this book. We chase after philosophies, religious ideals, and social codes of conduct. We chase after spirit. We chase after truth. We chase after beauty. But only the most well practiced habits of social intelligence allow the agents within any human swarm to wheel on a dime and improvise on the chase.

In order to hone such habits of mind, we need practice. It is easy to lose our way and to get separated from the creative pack unless we teach ourselves beforehand to intuitively chase after the kinds of stories that best serve our needs and aspirations as members of the human swarm. At the heart of any story worth chasing after, within the creative continuum you will likely find one or more of the following ten principles of creative learning and practice enticing you forward.

Principle 1:
Chase any habit wherein creativity generates novelty.

I never fail to find it remarkable that something I learned to do twenty to forty years ago is fresh and absolutely new and thrilling to a student in my classroom. Is creativity manifested as the totally novel solution to a newly presented problem, a solution that has never been seen before under the sun? No, that is obviously overstating the case. It is enough that the creator has never before conceived the approach taken in address of the problem. That is novelty enough to alter the next person's approach, and the next person after that. This is how a swarm of creative purpose often begins or is reinitiated.

Principle 2:
Chase any habit wherein creativity develops capacity.

Creativity's purpose is manifested when a problem is addressed one way the first time it is considered, only to be approached differently based on refined perceptions the second time it is approached. This develops a capacity to see things anew, resulting in a renewed approach often taken by a different agent within the creative swarm. In this way, a repertoire of approaches and solutions is typically developed and retained for future refinement within the social memory of the swarm; this capacity allows for any given swarm of social activity to create the means of its ongoing development.

Principle 3:
Chase any habit wherein creativity produces inquiry.
My mother used flash cards early on in my literacy development to drill my word recognition, and my literacy was further stimulated during my attendance of a community pre-kindergarten. But when I began reading during the summers as an elementary school student, my reading level accelerated by leaps and bounds. I became curious to know more. My questions might have been an annoyance to adults but they made me the learner I still am today. My questions prepared me to move in accord with other inquirers.

Principle 4:
Chase any habit wherein creativity initiates pathways.
Creativity's purpose is often merely to *initiate* an effective pathway toward a solution or question—a methodology—even if at the conclusion of the creator's effort, that pathway is only partially or preliminarily shaped. That is enough to serve as the starting point for another member of the creative swarm, or as a point of departure to be revisited by the initial pioneer.

Principle 5:
Chase any habit wherein creativity reinterprets conventions.
Creativity is geared toward the reinterpretation of conventional understandings or settled-upon points of view. A creative swarm depends on the diversity of its constituents to generate alternative ways of seeing the same information. As a relatively new nation, the United States of America grew to become a world leader in industry, invention and the arts more rapidly than thought possible because its diversity—the open invitation extended to displaced and oppressed masses across the world who wished to

enter and become new citizens, also fostered swarms of unprecedented creativity. Old world conventions of class and tradition were reinterpreted in the gumbo of the new world, giving birth not only to jazz, but to American optimism and innovation.

After its defeat in World War II, Japan grew to become a world leader in industry and invention so quickly because it was willing to incorporate Western economic and political principles, reinterpreting its old imperial conventions. Communist China, with its strange adoption of Western capitalism, has defied all conventions to become a major economic force on the world stage. Each is an example of collective creativity trumping the prevailing conventions and practices.

Wherever conventions are reinterpreted one also finds an entryway to the creative continuum.

Principle 6:
Chase any habit wherein creativity forecasts possibility.
Creativity allows us to perceive a point of view predicated not on the information at hand, but rather on information conveyed from afar from outlying members of the swarm. Let me offer a personal example. I never met Charles M. Schulz personally and he probably never visited my little neighborhood of Crown Heights in the borough of Brooklyn—a generally low-income community with a quirky blend of African Americans, Caribbean immigrants, Puerto Ricans, and black-garbed ultra-Orthodox Jews. Nevertheless, I recognized myself in Schulz's cartoons decades after he first put pen and ink to paper. As a shy youngster who found security in my daydreams as I was bussed everyday to a neighborhood a world away just to get an adequate education, I immediately recognized the loneliness of

Charlie Brown and the wild imagination of Snoopy. I knew I was not alone.

So I connected to Schulz and a hive of other visual artists I encountered. Drawings entered the realm of my possibility and began to flow from me; even when I couldn't find any words to say, or when I stammered over them, I was able to draw what I could not otherwise tell. I was engaged with a creative intelligence I did not initiate, yet which was destined to become my own as I entered the swarm. I certainly did not see it coming, but the possibilities before me as little boy were as suddenly as endless as the cavernous vaults and sub-basements within Snoopy's doghouse.

Principle 7:
Chase any habit wherein creativity increases complexity.
Creative practice takes both known and newly discovered elements of information and draws them into convergence to make a more complex network of meaning. The more complex and integrated the network, the more difficult it is to be rendered obsolete. Creative practices are the primary means by which we build collaborative forms and constructs, inform each other's thinking, and transform our known contexts. Metaphorical leaps are made in the midst of complexity, where everyday stories become transcendent, conveying meaning and validation no longer just for one, but for many.

Principle 8:
Chase any habit wherein creativity invites inclusivity.
In a creative swarm, one is free to supersede favored or well-traveled methodologies, viewing the creation of new pathways as

essential to the growing infrastructure of a social network. There is no "one best path." Even if there was, a pathway that works best for one individual may be inaccessible or less than advantageous for another. In the same way that we carve curb cuts into sidewalks and build ramps alongside buildings to assure that access is available to all of differing abilities, a creative continuum opens the way toward universally accessible learning opportunities.

Principle 9:
Chase any habit wherein creativity informs divergently.
Creativity's purpose is also to overwrite prior solutions and questions, diverging from prior thinking to present possibilities for filling in the gaps of knowledge along the way. The heterogeneity of the roles of the agents within a social network disrupts the sameness of outcomes.

Beware those who cry out against diversity. The greatest enemies to innovation are those whose goal is to build permanent roadblocks between diverse citizens or those working to become citizens, preventing folks of different mindsets and lifestyle habits from building mutually sustaining inroads toward greater understanding. Yes, our relationships are that important. All the animals at the watering hole are not the same. You don't have to be like-minded to be united. You simply have to be up to the chase. Unity of purpose among the "same" can be as mindless as a mob. Unity of purpose among the "different," however, demands dialogue that gives birth to new movements and more interesting conversations. This dialogue takes place in and around a continuum of learners. Learning makes new sense of prior knowledge and releases that newly acquired sense to the surrounding society for others to make sense of. This work is cyclical; we learn what others have learned and others learn what we learn, back and forth in a negotiation between socially attained knowledge and individually expressed knowledge.

Principle 10:
Chase any habit wherein creativity comes simply.
Follow the trail of the creative partner in front of you, and keep pace with the creative partner beside you. Look up in the sky at the migrating flock. At some point in the journey, every bird in the flock will rotate into the lead. A child makes up a funny story for his playmates to act out during school recess. A businesswoman tells an inspiring story to motivate other would-be entrepreneurs at a conference. A mineworker rallies his fellow laborers to unionize and protect themselves as they share harrowing stories of survival within an unjust, unsafe workplace environment. Out of such simple interactions, new creative solutions and new creative leaders emerge.

In summary of this concluding chapter, *you are the agent of the innovation you need—chase after the story you wish to become*. The force of creativity meanders. It morphs and shifts its periphery like an amoeba. It rushes ahead. But what does not change is the essential *purpose* of creativity. Its nucleus. The creative continuum offers stories to live by, to center our energies and offer up new possibilities for the other agents being served.

CREATIVITY CREATES CULTURE. EACH CULTURE, LARGE or small, is a part of a larger continuum—a complex pattern of human behaviors and practices, systemized to be self-sustaining and an incubator for the creativity of the human agents that constitute it. Ideally, our school and workplace cultures are the coalescing of myriad independent and decentralized choices—the chaos of life rendered into coherent pattern through the assembly of meaningful marks, models, scientific and aesthetic interventions, along with other new and revisited experiential stories. The stories we choose to live by serve as biocultural mechanisms, or enticements, for rapidly altering the development or direction of each human swarm we belong to. And within a creative continuum, at the very end of the stories we live by, we find the start of the stories we have inexorably become.

NOTES

INTRODUCTION: ANCIENT SECRET SOCIETIES AND SNOOPY'S DOGHOUSE

1. Public Radio International, "Can Creativity Be Measured with a Score?," November 6, 2012, http://www.pri.org/ stories/arts-entertainment/arts/ can-creativity-be-measured-with-a-score-12193.html. The abbreviated article features an audio highlight from PRI's Peabody Award–winning WYNC radio show *Studio 360 with Kurt Andersen*, on what's happening in pop culture and the arts.

2. Douglas Eby, "Improvising Creativity," accessed January 12, 2013, http:// blogs.psychcentral.com/creative-mind/2012/04/improvising-creativity/.

3. From the Biblical reference in Genesis 1:28: "And God blessed them, and God said unto them, Be fruitful, and multiply, and replenish the earth..."

4. Frank Lewis Dyer and Thomas Commerford Martin, *Edison: His Life and Inventions Vol. 1* (New York and London: Harper & Brothers Publishers, 1910), 264.

5. From the familiar anecdote often attributed to Ralph Waldo Emerson, "Build a better mousetrap and the world will beat a path to your door," but which is actually from an 1889 anthology called Borrowings by Sarah Yule and Mary Keene, in which Emerson's original quotation was revised substantially.

6. Andrew B. Hargadon and Yellowlees Douglas, "When Innovations Meet Institutions: Edison and the Design of the Electric Light," *Administrative Science Quarterly* 46, no. 3 (2001): 476–501; 477.

7. Ibid., 477n.

8. Robert E. Conot, *A Streak of Luck* (New York: Seaview Books, 1979), 469.

9. Robert Boyd and Peter J. Richerson, *Culture and the Evolutionary Process* (Chicago: University of Chicago Press, 1985), 2.

10. See A. D. Efland, *Art and Cognition: Integrating the Visual Arts in the Curriculum* (New York: Teachers College Press & Reston, VA: National Art Education Association, 2002).

11. See P. Miller, *The Smart Swarm: How Understanding Flocks, Schools, and Colonies Can Make Us Better at Communicating, Decision Making, and Getting Things Done* (New York: Avery, 2010).

12. C. J. Lumsden and E. O. Wilson, *Genes, Mind, and Culture: The Coevolutionary Process* (Cambridge, MA: Harvard University Press, 1981), 7. See also J. Lopreato, *Human Nature and Biocultural Evolution* (Boston: Allen and Unwin, 1984).

13. See L. Fisher, *The Perfect Swarm: The Science of Complexity in Everyday Life* (New York: Basic Books, 2009). See also Miller, *The Smart Swarm*.

14. Po Bronson and Ashley Merryman, "The Creativity Crisis," *Newsweek*, July 10, 2010, http://www.thedaily beast.com/newsweek/2010/07/10/the-creativity-crisis.html.

15. Linda Kreger Silverman, PhD, "At-Risk Youth and the Creative Process," *Visual-Spatial Resource*, p. 2, accessed March 30, 2013, http://www.visual spatial.org/files/atrisk.pdf.

16. Michael G. Vaughn, Jade Wexler, Kevin M. Beaver, Brian E. Perron, Gregory Roberts, and Qiang Fu, "Psychiatric Correlates of Behavioral Indicators of School Disengagement in the United States," *Psychiatr Q.* 82, no. 3 (September 2011): 191–206. According to the 2010 online study, which presents a statistical analysis on this subject, "school dropout shows that it is typically a gradual process of disengaging or disconnecting from school both physically and mentally."

17. This quote is from a recently released report by the President's Committee on the Arts and Humanities: "The European Union (EU) has recognized the critical importance of creativity in education. As part of the European Year of Creativity in 2009, teachers in the 27 member countries were surveyed about their perspectives and over 95% of teacher respondents believe that creativity is a fundamental competence to be developed in school and is applicable to all subject areas. Sixty percent of EU teachers indicated they had received training in innovative pedagogies and 40% directly in creativity." M. C. Dwyer, *Reinvesting in Arts Education: Winning America's Future through Creative Schools* (Washington, DC: President's Committee on the Arts and the Humanities, May 2011), 38.

18. In a report titled *Are They Really Ready to Work?*, several organizations have collaborated to produce an in-depth study on the levels of educational preparedness attained by new entrants into the U.S. workforce. The authors of this report surveyed corporations, ascertaining that while

employers count on employees with a comprehensive knowledge base, they also place great value on "applied skills such as problem solving, collaboration and creativity, as critical for success in the workplace." Dwyer, *Reinvesting in Arts Education*, 29. See also J. Casner-Lotto and M. W. Benner, *Are They Really Ready to Work? Employers' Perspectives on the Basic Knowledge and Applied Skills of New Entrants to the 21st Century U.S. Workforce* (New York, NY: The Conference Board, the Partnership for 21st Century Skills, Corporate Voices for Working Families, and the Society for Human Resource Management, 2006).

19. J. Lichtenberg, C. Woock, and M. Wright, *Ready to Innovate: Are Educators and Executives Aligned on the Creative Readiness of the U.S. Workforce?* (New York: Conference Board, 2008).

20. National Center on Education and the Economy, *Tough Choices or Tough Times: The Report of the New Commission on the Skills of the American Workforce* (San Francisco: Jossey-Bass, 2006).

21. National Assembly of State Arts Agencies, n.d.

22. A report by the President's Committee on the Arts and Humanities summarizes the challenge and the opportunity at hand. According to the report, "the arts are a vital part of the culture and life of this country, and all students deserve access to the arts in school as part of a complete education." The report charges that in the same way "science and social studies are deemed essential subjects independent of their value to other learning outcomes, the arts merit a similar unambiguous place in the curriculum," The report aims to spur a new reinvestment in arts education as a research-tested means to "motivate and engage students; stimulate curiosity and foster creativity; teach 21st Century Skills such as problem solving and team work; and facilitate school-wide collaborations." *Reinvesting in Arts Education: Winning America's Future through Creative Schools*, May 4, 2011, p. 48, http://www.pcah.gov/sites/default/files/PCAH_Reinvesting_4web_0.pdf.

23. Cited in Dwyer, *Reinvesting in Arts Education*, 13.

CHAPTER ONE: HOW TO UNDERDEVELOP CREATIVITY

1. "Tom Kelley (Founder–Ideo)—"Orbiting the Giant Hairball," YouTube, accessed April 3, 2013, at https://www.youtube.com/watch?v=YV-80priPm0.

2. Andrew Grant and Gaia Grant's experiment, "Hands Up Part I: 'How Creative Are You?'" YouTube, accessed April 3, 2013, at https://www.youtube.com/watch?v=MhBIiNl3edk.

3. Herbert M. Kliebard, *Schooled to Work: Vocationalism and the American Curriculum, 1876–1946* (New York: Teachers College Press, 1999), 43.

4. Bernadette M. Baker, *In Perpetual Motion: Theories of Power, Educational History, and the Child* (Berne, Switzerland: Peter Lang, 2001), 428.

5. Ibid., 501.

6. Ibid., 496–97.

7. Raymond E. Callahan, *Education and the Cult of Efficiency* (Chicago: University of Chicago Press, 1962), 14.

8. Ibid., 17.

9. Ibid., 15.

10. Ibid., 28.

11. Ibid.

12. John D. Philbrick, *City School Systems in the United States* (Washington, DC: U.S. Bureau of Education, 1885), 47.

13. Callahan, *Education and the Cult of Efficiency*, 27.

14. Baker, *In Perpetual Motion*, 501.

15. Ibid., 496.

16. Ibid., 497.

17. Ibid., 494.

18. Ibid., 428.

19. Ibid., 494, 495.

20. Ashis Nandy, *The Intimate Enemy: The Loss and Recovery of Self Under Colonialism* (Delhi: Oxford University Press, 1983), x.

21. First argued by author Daniel Pink and cited in Katherine Bell, "The MFA is the New MBA," *Harvard Business Review*, April 14, 2008, http://blogs.hbr.org/cs/2008/04/the_mfa_is_the_new_mba.html.

CHAPTER TWO: SOCIAL NETWORKS

1. Cited in R. S. Prawat, "Dewey, Peirce, and the Learning Paradox," *American Educational Research Journal* 36, no. 1 (1999): 47–76; 48.

2. Ibid., 48.

3. "Motown Records: The Motown Story," *Randy's Rodeo*, accessed January 29, 2013, http://randysrodeo.com/features/motown/index.php.

4. Gilbert Cruz, "A Brief History of Motown," *Time*, January 12, 2009, http://www.time.com/time/arts/article/0,8599,1870975,00.html.

5. "Motown Records."

6. P. Miller, *The Smart Swarm: How Understanding Flocks, Schools, and Colonies Can Make Us Better at Communicating, Decision Making, and Getting Things Done* (New York: Avery, 2010), 10.

7. Jeff Cobb, "10 Lessons from the Swarm," *Mission to Learn: Life-Learning Blog*, October 10, 2010, http://www.missiontolearn.com/2010/10/smart-swarm/.

8. Ibid.

9. Ibid.

10. Miller, *The Smart Swarm*, 267.

11. Ibid., 49.

12. "Leonardo Da Vinci," *Wikipedia*, accessed February 4, 2013, http://en.wikipedia.org/wiki/Leonardo_da_Vinci.

13. Cobb, "10 Lessons from the Swarm."

14. Miller, *The Smart Swarm*, 39.

15. K. L. Carroll, "Researching Paradigms in Art Education," in S. D. La Pierre and E. Zimmerman (eds.), *Research Methods and Methodologies for Art Education* (Reston, VA: National Art Education Association, 1997), 171–192; 171.

16. See T. S. Kuhn, *The Structure of Scientific Revolutions, 3rd ed.* (Chicago: The University of Chicago Press, 1962/1996).

17. Carroll, "Researching Paradigms in Art Education," 174.

18. J. Henry, *The Scientific Revolution and Origins of Modern Science, 2nd ed.* (New York: Palgrave, 2002), 4.

19. J. Berger, *Ways of Seeing* (London: Penguin Books, 1972).

20. A quote by Claude Lévi-Strauss in Berger, *Ways of Seeing*, 86.

CHAPTER THREE: SYSTEMS

1. Online excerpt by Keith Sawyer, *Group Genius: The Creative Power of Collaboration*, accessed March 31, 2013, http://www.artsci.wustl.edu/~ksawyer/groupgenius/excerpt.html.

2. G. Lindsay, "Working Beyond the Cube," *Fast Company*, March 2013, 36.

3. D. H. Meadows, *Thinking in Systems: A Primer* (White River Junction, VT: Chelsea Green Publishing Company, 2008), 188.

4. Ibid., 11, 12.

5. Ibid., 25.

6. Ibid., 17.

7. Cited in Marvin Harris, *Cannibals and Kings: The Origins of Culture* (New York: Random House, 1977), 170–71.

8. Ibid., 172.

9. Eugene F. Rice, Jr., *The Foundations or Early Modern Europe, 1460–1559* (New York: Norton, 1970), 58.

10. Ibid., 60.

11. Ibid., 32.

12. Ibid., 47.

13. Ibid., 37.

14. See Tzvetan Todorov, *The Conquest of America: The Question of the Other*, trans. Richard Howard (New York: Harper & Row, 1984).

15. From the writings of John H. Van Evrie, *White Supremacy and Negro Subordination* (New York: Van Evrie, Horton & Co, 1868), cited in Sunand Tryambak Joshi, ed., *Documents of American Prejudice* (New York: Basic Books, 1999), 293.

CHAPTER FOUR: SWARMS

1. "Shell, OPEC and the Price of Oil," *11 Changes*, accessed March 2, 2013, http://www.11changes.com/scenario-planning/where-it-all-started-the-best-known-example.html. The article describes the history and benefits of scenario planning.

2. "Skunk Works," *Wikipedia*, accessed March 3, 2013, http://en.wikipedia.org/wiki/Skunk_Works.

3. "Skunkworks Project," *Wikipedia*, accessed March 3, 2013, http://en.wikipedia.org/wiki/Skunkworks_project.

4. H. Pearse, "Brother, Can You Spare a Paradigm?: The Theory Beneath the Practice," *Studies in Art Education* 24, no. 3 (1983): 158–63; 159.

5. See M. A. Stankiewicz, *Roots of Art Education Practice* (Worcester, MA: Davis Publication, Inc., 2001). See also j. jagodzinski, "A Para-Critical /Sitical/Sightical Reading of Ralph Smith's Excellence in Art Education," *Journal of Social Theory in Art Education* 11 (1991): 119–59.

6. Pearse, "Brother, Can You Spare a Paradigm?," 160.

7. M. B. Cancienne and C. N. Snowber, "Writing Rhythm: Movement as Method," *Qualitative Inquiry* 9, no. 2 (2003): 237–53; 238.

8. Pearse, "Brother, Can You Spare a Paradigm?," 161.

9. G. Ladson-Billings, "It's Your World, I'm Just Trying to Explain It: Understanding Our Epistemological and Methodological Challenges," *Qualitative Inquiry* 9, no. 1 (2003): 5–12; 11.

10. Grace Elizabeth Hale, *Making Whiteness: The Culture of Segregation in the South, 1890–1940* (New York: Vintage, 1998), 7.

11. James D. Anderson, *The Education of Blacks in the South, 1860–1935* (Chapel Hill: University of North Carolina Press, 1988), 2.

12. David B. Tyack, *The One Best System: A History of American Urban Education* (Cambridge: Harvard University Press, 1974), 121.

13. Herbert M. Kliebard, *Schooled to Work: Vocationalism and the American Curriculum, 1876–1946* (New York: Teachers College Press, 1999), 14.

14. Ibid., 224.

15. See Michael D. Harris, *Colored Pictures: Race and Visual Representation* (Chapel Hill: The University of North Carolina Press, 2003). See also Deborah Willis, *Reflections in Black: A History of Black Photographers, 1840 to the Present* (New York: W. W. Norton & Co., 2000).

16. See *Fact vs. Fiction*, a New York Times Arts Interactive Feature, accessed September 15, 2008, http://www.nytimes.com/packages/khtml/2007/05/10/arts/20070511_SCHOMBURG_FEATURE.html.

17. Willis, *Reflections in Black*, 36.

18. Ibid.

19. "The Art of Romare Bearden: A Resource for Teachers," p. 34, accessed June 16, 2013, http://www.nga.gov/ content/dam/ngaweb/Education/learning-resources/teaching-packets/pdfs/bearden-tchpk.pdf. This is an online teaching resource packet on the life of artist Romare Bearden.

20. Alain Locke, ed., *The New Negro* (New York: Touchstone, 1925/1992), 4.

21. "Six Sigma," *Wikipedia*, accessed March 6, 2013, http://en.wikipedia.org/wiki/Six_Sigma.

22. D. Boorstein, *How to Change the World: Social Entrepreneurs and the Power of New Ideas* (New York: Oxford University Press, 2004).

23. Tom Vanden Brook, "Parks Courage Changed Nation," *USA Today*, October 25, 2005, http://usatoday30.usatoday.com/news/nation/2005–10

–24-parksdetailedobit_x.htm. The article was written to memorialize Mrs. Rosa Parks on the occasion of her death in October 2005.

CHAPTER FIVE: SUPERORGANISMS

1. "Superorganism," *Wikipedia*, accessed March 3, 2013, http://en.wikipedia. org/wiki/Superorganism.

2. Aubrey D. N. J. de Grey, "Life Span Extension Research and Public Debate: Societal Considerations," *Studies in Ethics, Law, and Technology* 1, no. 1 (2007): 1. Published by the Methuselah Foundation.

3. E. W. Eisner, *The Arts and the Creation of Mind* (New Haven & London: Yale University Press, 2002), xi.

4. M. A. Stankiewicz, "A Dangerous Business: Visual Culture Theory and Education Policy," *Arts Education Policy Review* 105, no. 6 (2004): 5–13.

5. P. Duncum, "Art Education for New Times," *Studies in Art Education* 38, no. 2 (1997): 69–79; 69.

6. A. Wright, *Glut: Mastering Information through the Ages* (Washington, DC: Joseph Henry Press, 2007), 6.

7. Some of my ideas are detailed in "Art Education as a Network for Curriculum Innovation and Adaptable Learning," *Advocacy White Papers for Art Education, Section 1: What High-Quality Art Education Provides* (Reston, VA: National Art Education Association, 2011), http://www.art-educators.org/advocacy/whitepapers.

8. For more information, visit "One Laptop per Child" website, http://one. laptop.org.

9. From the final soliloquy of replicant Roy Batty as he dies in the classic film *Blade Runner*. More information about this soliloquy and its lasting cinematic impact is detailed at http://en.wikipedia.org/wiki/Tears_in_rain_soliloquy.

10. D. W. Stinson, *African American Male Students and Achievement in School Mathematics: A Critical Postmodern Analysis of Agency* (Unpublished doctoral dissertation, Athens, GA: Georgia State University, 2004), 57.

11. O. Gude, "Art Education for Democratic Life," *Art Education* 62, no. 6 (2009): 6–11; 7–8.

12. D. H. Meadows, *Thinking in Systems: A Primer* (White River Junction, VT: Chelsea Green Publishing Company, 2008), 12.

13. B. Peach, ed., *Richard Price and the Ethical Foundations of the American Revolution* (Durham, NC: Duke University Press, 1979), 67.

14. J. Drew, "Cultural Composition: Stuart Hall on Ethnicity and the Discursive Turn," *JAC* 18, no. 1 (1998): 171–96; 173.

15. Find out more about the important film *Precious Knowledge* at http://www.preciousknowledgefilm.com/.

16. Find out more about the film *Dark Girls* at http://officialdarkgirlsmovie.com/.

17. Cited on a blog posting about the aftermath of this social entrepreneurship venture. Find out more about this film at the Waste Land's official website: http://www.wastelandmovie.com/.

18. J. M. Wilson, "Art-Making Behavior: Why and How Arts Education Is Central to Learning," *Art Education Policy Review* 99, no. 6 (1998): 26–33; 29.

19. Ibid., 32.

20. Nicole Carter, "A Start-Up to Create 23 Million Jobs in America?" *Inc.*, January 9, 2012, http://www.inc.com/nicole-carter/start-up-to-create-23-million-jobs.html.

21. More information about crowdfunding and its variations can be found at http://en.wikipedia.org/wiki/Crowd_funding.

22. More information about Professor Muhammad Yunus and the Grameen Bank may be found at http://www.muhammadyunus.org/index.php/yunus-centre/about-yunus-centre.

CHAPTER SIX: STORIES

1. Stephen Fry, "Living with Harry Potter," interview with J. K. Rowling, broadcast on BBC Radio4, December 10, 2005. The transcript can be found at http://www.accio-quote.org/articles/2005/1205.-bbc-fry.html.

2. "*Harry Potter* Influences and Analogues," *Wikipedia*, accessed April 20, 2013, http://en.wikipedia.org/wiki/Harry_Potter_influences_and_analogues. The article discusses literary sources that influenced J. K. Rowling's writing of *Harry Potter*.

3. H. McEwan and K. Egan, eds., *Narrative in Teaching, Learning, and Research* (New York: Teachers College Press, 1995), x.

4. See B. Bettelheim, *The Uses of Enchantment: The Meaning and Importance of Fairy Tales* (New York: Vintage Books, 1989).

5. McEwan and Egan, *Narrative in Teaching, Learning, and Research*, xi.

6. Abigail Tucker, "Jack Andraka, the Teen Prodigy of Pancreatic Cancer," *Smithsonian*, December 2012, http://www.smithsonianmag.com/science-nature/Jack-Andraka-the-Teen-Prodigy-of-Pancreatic-Cancer-179996151.html.

7. Jeffrey Kluger, "Shhh! Genius At Work," *Time*, April 12, 2012, http://healthland.time.com/2012/04/12/shhh-genius-at-work/.

8. M. Turner, *The Literary Mind: The Origins of Thought and Language* (New York: Oxford University Press, 1996), 7.

9. Ibid., 22. Emphasis in original.

10. M. Johnson, *The Body in the Mind: The Bodily Basics of Meaning, Imagination and Reason* (Chicago: University of Chicago Press, 1987), 79. Emphasis in original.

11. Bronwyn Davies, *(In)scribing Body/Landscape Relations* (Walnut Creek, California: AltaMira Press, 2000), 43.

12. T. Siler, *Breaking the Mind Barrier: The Artscience of Neurocosmology* (New York: Touchstone, 1990), 28–29.

13. G. Lakoff, *Women, Fire and Dangerous Things: What Categories Reveal about the Mind* (Chicago: University of Chicago Press, 1987), 276.

14. Turner, *The Literary Mind*, 60.

15. Scott Barry Kaufman, "Why Daydreamers Are More Creative," *Huffington Post*, February 27, 2011, http://www.huffingtonpost.com/scott-barry-kaufman/creativity-brain_b_827763.html.

16. Ibid.

17. J. E. Dowling, *Creating Mind: How the Brain Works* (New York: W. W. Norton & Company, 1998), 13.

18. Jonah Lehrer titled, "Bother Me, I'm Thinking," February 19, 2011, http://online.wsj.com/article/SB10001424052748703584804576144192132144506.html.

19. Kaufman, "Why Daydreamers Are More Creative."

20. C. Geertz, *Local Knowledge: Further Essays in Interpretive Anthropology* (New York: Basic Books, 1983), 99.

21. Jerome Brooks, "Chinua Achebe, The Art of Fiction, No. 139," *The Paris Review*, interview with Chinua Achebe in 1994, online reprint, accessed March 23, 2013, http://www.theparisreview.org/interviews/1720/the-art-of-fiction-no-139-chinua-achebe.

22. Jane Yolen, "America's Cinderella," *Children's Literature in Education* 8, no. 1 (1977): 21–29. See also Mary Ann Nelson, *A Comparative Anthology of Children's Literature* (New York: Holt, Rinehart & Winston, 1972).

23. See J. H. Rolling, *Cinderella Story: A Scholarly Sketchbook about Race, Identity, Barack Obama, the Human Spirit, and Other Stuff that Matters* (Lanham, MD: AltaMira Press, 2010).

24. Ibid.

25. Malin Grunberg Banyasz, "The Newark Earthworks," *Archaeology*, January 22, 2010, http://archive.archaeology.org/online/features/hopewell/.

26. Ibid. According to the article, "[t]he Newark Earthworks was one of 14 sites nominated in January 2008 by the Department of Interior for submission by the United States to the UNESCO World Heritage List."

27. W. James, *The Principles of Psychology, vol. 1* (New York: Henry Holt, 1890), 288.

28. R. McKee, *Story: Substance, Structure, Style, and the Principles of Screenwriting* (New York: HarperCollins, 1997), 5.

CHAPTER SEVEN: SCHOOLS

1. An excerpt from the program overview, *Research Symposium of the Alliance for the Arts in Research Universities*, March 2013, p. 1.

2. Online press release issued by Penn State's College of Arts and Architecture announcing Penn State's hosting of the March 2013 Research Symposium of the Alliance for the Arts in Research Universities, accessed April 26, 2013, https://artsandarchitecture.psu.edu/news/penn-stateplays-key-role-alliance-arts-research-universities.

3. An excerpt from the transcript of a recent speech by Diane Ravitch. Valerie Strauss, "Whose Children Have Been Left Behind? Framing the 2012 Ed Debate," *Washington Post*, January 3, 2012, http://www.washingtonpost.com/blogs/answer-sheet/post/whose-children-have-been-left-behind-framing-the-2012-ed-debate/2012/01/02/gIQAz3nDXP_blog.html.

4. B. M. Baker, *In Perpetual Motion: Theories of Power, Educational History, and the Child* (New York: Peter Lang, 2001), 496, 497.

5. J. Dewey, *Democracy and Education: An Introduction to the Philosophy of Education* (New York: Free Press, 1916/1966), 46.

6. H. Cuffaro, *Experimenting with the World: John Dewey and the Early Childhood Classroom* (New York: Teachers College Press, 1995), 19.

7. See J. H. Rolling, "Who Is at the City Gates? A Surreptitious Approach to Curriculum-making in Art Education," *Art Education* 59, no. 6 (2006): 40–46.

8. Renee Hobbs, "Improvisation and Strategic Risk Taking in Informal Learning in Digital Media Literacy," doi:10.1080/17439884.2013.75651. The entire article is is available for download at http://mediaeducationlab. com/sites/mediaeducationlab.com/files/Hobbs,%20Improvisation%20 and%20Strategic%20Risk%20Taking.pdf.

9. J. Spring, *The American School: 1642–2000, 5th ed.* (New York: McGraw-Hill, 2001), 31, 32.

10. "More Lessons About Charter Schools," *New York Times*, February 1, 2013, http://www.nytimes. com/2013/02/02/opinion/more-lessons-about-charter-schools.html?_r=0.

11. P. Miller, *The Smart Swarm: How Understanding Flocks, Schools, and Colonies Can Make Us Better at Communicating, Decision Making, and Getting Things Done* (New York: Avery, 2010), 42.

12. Ibid., 43.

13. Anu Partanen, "What Americans Keep Ignoring about Finland's School Success," *The Atlantic*, December 29, 2011, http://www.theatlantic.com/national/archive/2011/12/what-americanskeep-ignoring-about-finlands-school-success/250564/.

14. Ibid.

15. Ibid.

16. Ibid.

17. Ibid.

18. Video illustrating a talk by author Daniel Pink, "RSA Animate—Drive: The Surprising Truth About What Motivates Us," YouTube, accessed April 20, 2013, http://www.youtube.com/watch?v=u6XAPnuFjJc&list=PL39BF9545D740ECFF.

CHAPTER EIGHT: RETHINKING CREATIVITY

1. Bill McKibben, *Dance of the Honeybee*, video journal segment on *Moyers & Company*, April 19, 2013, http://billmoyers.com/segment/%E2%80%9Cdance-of-the-honey-bee%E2%80%9D/.

2. From website of the National Resources Defense Council (NRDC) along with a more extensive list of the many fruit, nut, vegetable, and field crops pollinated by honeybees. "Vanishing Bees," National Resource Defense Council, accessed April 24, 2013, http://www. nrdc.org/wildlife/animals/bees.asp.

3. W. F. Pinar, *What Is Curriculum Theory?* (Mahwah, NJ: Lawrence Erlbaum Associates, Inc, 2004), 35.

4. P. Slattery, *Curriculum Development in the Postmodern Era* (New York & London: Garland Publishing, Inc., 1995), 77.

5. M. Polanyi, *The Tacit Dimension* (New York: Anchor Books, 1967), 4.

6. B. Wilson, "The Second Search: Metaphor, Dimensions of Meaning, and Research in Art Education," in S. La Pierre and E. Zimmerman, eds., *Research Methods and Methodology for Art Education* (Reston, VA: National Art Education Association, 1997), 1.

7. W. J. T. Mitchell, *Iconology: Image, Text, Ideology* (Chicago: University of Chicago Press, 1986), 67.

8. From Pam Lawton, in a personal communication, February 12, 2006.

9. Ibid.

10. From a written reflection by Nyasa, a third-grade student, Spring 2005.

11. From a written reflection by Shiva, a fourth-grade student, Spring 2005.

12. J. H. Rolling, "Marginalia and Meaning: Offsite/sight/cite Points of Reference for Extended Trajectories in Learning," *Journal of Social Theory in Art Education* 26 (2006a): 224, 225.

13. Ibid.

14. From a written reflection by Tal, a third-grade student, Spring 2005.

15. D. Novitz, Art, Narrative, and Human Nature," in L. P. Hinchman and S. K. Hinchman, eds., *Memory, Identity, Community: The Idea of Narrative in the Human Sciences* (Albany: State University of New York Press, 2001), 158.

16. J. Dewey, *Human Nature and Conduct* (New York: Modern Library, 1930), 37.

17. H. Cuffaro, *Experimenting with the World: John Dewey and the Early Childhood Classroom* (New York: Teachers College Press, 1995), 21.

18. Dewey, *Human Nature and Conduct*, 88.

19. The concept of "expanded pedagogy" is discussed in S. Bey, "Aaron Douglas and Hale Woodruff: African American Art Education, Gallery

Work, and Expanded Pedagogy," *Studies in Art Education* 52, no. 2 (2011): 112–26.

20. See the work of B. Wilson, "More Lessons from the Superheroes of J. C. Holz: The Visual Culture of Childhood and the Third Pedagogical Site," *Art Education* 58, no. 6 (2005): 18–34.

INDEX